KNITTED SCARVES AND COWLS

30 STYLISH DESIGNS TO KNIT

JODY LONG

Tuva Publishing
www.tuvapublishing.com

Address Merkez Mah. Cavusbasi Cad. No:71
Cekmekoy - Istanbul 34782 / Turkey
Tel: +9 0216 642 62 62

Knitted Scarves and Cowls

First Print 2017 / July

All Global Copyrights Belong To
Tuva Tekstil ve Yayıncılık Ltd.

Content Knitting

Editor in Chief Ayhan DEMİRPEHLİVAN

Project Editor Kader DEMİRPEHLİVAN

Designer Jody LONG

Technical Editors Leyla ARAS, Büşra ESER

Graphic Designers Ömer ALP, Abdullah BAYRAKÇI,
Zilal ÖNEL

Photograph Tuva Publishing, Yevhen SMALTSUGA

Models Valeriia GERASYMOVA, Valeriia HOLOVA,
Daria ZAGREBELNA, Eliza PROJEIKO and Oleg TINTUL

ISBN 978-605-9192-28-6

Printing House
Bilnet Matbaacılık ve Yayıncılık A.Ş.

TuvaYayincilik TuvaPublishing
TuvaYayincilik TuvaPublishing

This book is dedicated to my mum Elaine for the unforgettable help!

This publication would not have been possible without the following:

Susan Winn for her all round essential input into my projects and writing the captions. The models **Valeriia Gerasymova, Valeriia Holova, Daria Zagrebelna, Eliza Projeiko** and **Oleg Tintul**, from Gera Modeling Agency. **Vladyslav Ursatiy** who kindly transported me and my large suitcases to the shoot, to and from Kiev airport. **Yevhen Smaltsuga** for the great photography. My mother **Elaine Long** and sister **Kaylie Long** for sending yarn and organising knitters. The fantastic knitters who have produced beautifully knitted garments under deadline pressure! **Sheila Riley, Paulette Burgess, Janet May, Tina Miller, Claire Wightman, Paula Paynter, Nikki Ingham, Caroline Bletsis, Mary Alderton, Denise Beckerleg, Emily Collier, Sam Clarke** and **Andrea Brown**. A special thank you to the amazing team at Tuva Publishing, whose enthusiasm is inspiring.

introduction

If you are looking for that special something to make as a gift for a loved one, or a simple shawl for the winter walks then you are sure to find something within this collection.

Jody has created for every season and all tastes. Wear the frilly scarf on (page 30) for a stroll along the beach, or the two tonal fair isle flower scarf on (page 64) to the theatre over a dress to make a real statement.

There is plenty for the guys too, the checkered cowl on (page 46) will look great worn casually.

Happy Knitting!

Jody Long

contents

SCARVES

gallery of scarves

P.112

P.78

P.68

P.34

P.76

P.102

P.72

P.120

P.98

P.100

P.64

P.52

P.126

P.50

P.122

P.92

P.60

P.46

P.116

P.110

P.90

P.48

P.30

P.86

P.96

P.42

P.56

P.38

P.82

P.106

EQUIPMENTS

The pattern will tell you at the start what equipment is required to knit the project. The most important purchase is that of the knitting needles. These come in a range of diameters, which are either described in metric millimetres or by one of two sizing systems. Check the pattern carefully and if you are unsure, ask in the store before purchasing. However, the pattern will give a suggested size only to achieve the correct number of stitches and rows in a given distance.

KNITTING NEEDLES
The type used in this book are made from bamboo and are ideal for all types of knitter's because they are light and the stitches are less likely to slide off them than with metal needles.

Check the needles carefully before buying to make sure there is no pitting in the surface and that the points are round and smooth. A longer point is useful on finer sizes. We recommend using Clover knitting needles.

CIRCULAR NEEDLES
Circular needles or "circs" as we lovingly call them, are simply two knitting tips joined by a flexible cord. Use them just as you would straight needles. The big advantage to circular needles is you can knit seamlessly in the round making them perfect for hats, they're much longer too which is great if you need lots of stitches and a straight needle just won't do! We recommend using Clover circular needles.

DOUBLE-POINTED NEEDLES
Double-pointed needles also known as DPNs are pointed at both ends of the needle. They are most useful when working smaller projects like i-cords, hat crowns and socks. Like the circular needles they are great for working in the round and making projects seamless. We recommend using Clover double-pointed needles.

CABLE NEEDLE
This is used for holding stitches to one side while others are being worked within a repeat. Look for a cable needle with a bend in it because it holds the stitches more securely.

STITCH HOLDERS
These prevent stitches from unraveling when not in use. Alternatively, a spare knitting needle of the same size or less (ideally double pointed) can be used as a stitch holder. For holding just a few stitches, a safety pin is always useful.

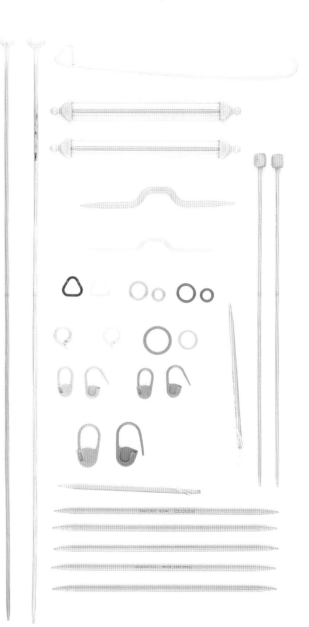

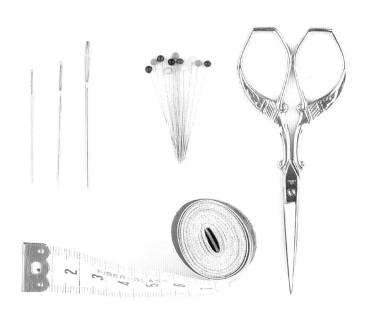

RULER
A plastic or metal ruler is less likely to become distorted and is useful to check the gauge (tension).

TAPE MEASURE
Useful for greater distances and checking project measurements.

SEWING NEEDLES
These should be blunt and round-pointed with a large eye. A sharp-pointed needle is more likely to split the yarn and/or stitches and result in an uneven seam.

SCISSORS
Always use a nice sharp-pointed pair for easy precise cutting of the yarn.

PINS
Always use large glass/plastic-headed pins so they can be seen and not be left in a knitted garment.

YARN INFORMATION
We have used only natural yarns that are soft and most importantly machine washable.

Below you will find all the information about the yarns used within this book, both qualities are available in a large color palette.

DMC WOOLLY is a natural 100% merino wool yarn that has a length of 136yd (125m) per 1.75oz (50g) ball.

DMC NATURA JUST COTTON MEDIUM is a 100% cotton yarn that has a length of 82yd (75m) per 1.75oz (50g) ball.

DMC NATURA JUST COTTON XL is a 100% cotton yarn that has a length of 82yd (75m) per 3.5oz (100g) ball.

INFORMATION

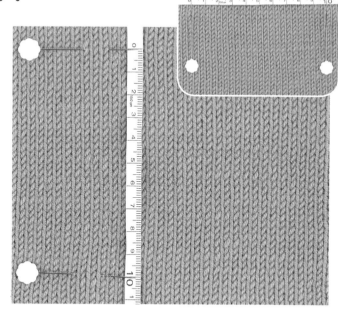

GAUGE (TENSION)

Obtaining the correct tension is perhaps the single factor which can make the difference between a successful garment and a disastrous one. It controls both the shape and size of an article, so any variation, however slight, can distort the finished garment. We recommend that you knit a square in pattern and/or stockinette (stocking) stitch (depending on the pattern instructions) of perhaps 5 - 10 more stitches and 5 - 10 more rows than those given in the tension note.

Mark out the central 4in (10cm) square with pins. If you have too many stitches to 4in (10cm) try again using thicker needles, if you have too few stitches to 4in (10cm) try again using finer needles.

Once you have achieved the correct tension your garment will be knitted to the measurements indicated in the pattern.

CASTING ON

Although there are many different techniques for casting on stitches, we recommend the long-tail cast on method (see page 15) for details.

STOCKINETTE (STOCKING) STITCH

Alternate one row knit and one row purl. The knit side is the right side of the work unless otherwise stated in the instructions.

GARTER STITCH

Knit every row. Both sides are the same and look identical.

K1, P1 RIB

Alternate one knit stitch with one purl stitch to the end of the row. On the next row, knit all the knit stitches and purl all the purl stitches as they face you.

SEED (MOSS) STITCH

Alternate one knit stitch with one purl stitch to the end of the row. On the next row, knit all the purl stitches and purl and the knit stitches as they face you.

INSTRUCTIONS IN ROUNDED BRACKETS

These are to be repeated the number of times stated after the closing bracket.

INSTRUCTIONS IN SQUARE BRACKETS

The instructions are given for the smallest size just before the opening of the bracket. Where they vary, work the figures in brackets for the larger sizes. One set of figures refer to all sizes.

JOINING YARN

Always join yarn at the beginning of a new row (unless you're working the Fair Isle or Intarsia method), and never knot the yarns as the knot may come through to the right side and spoil your work. Any long loose ends will be useful for sewing up afterwards.

WORKING STRIPES

When knitting different-colored stripes, carry yarns loosely up the side of your work.

FAIR ISLE METHOD

When two or three colors are worked repeatedly across a row, strand the yarn not in use loosely behind the stitches being worked. Always spread the stitches to their correct width to keep them elastic. It is advisable not to carry the stranded or 'floating' yarns over more than three stitches at a time, but weave them under and over the color you are working. The 'floating' yarns are therefore caught at the back of the work.

WORKING A LACE PATTERN

When working a lace pattern it is important to rememberer that if you are unable to work both the increase and corresponding decrease and vice versa, the stitches should be worked in stockinette (stocking) stitch.

WORKING FROM A CHART

Each square on a chart represents a stitch and a line of squares a row of knitting. Alongside the chart there will be a color and/or stitch key. When working from the charts, read odd rows (knit) from right to left and even rows (purl) from left to right, unless otherwise stated.

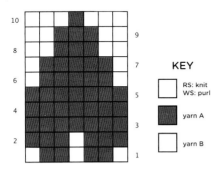

KEY

□	RS: knit WS: purl
■	yarn A
□	yarn B

SEAMS

After working for hours knitting a garment, it seems a great pity that many garments are spoiled because such little care is taken in the pressing and finishing process. Follow the text below for a truly professional-looking garment.

PRESSING

Block out each piece of knitting and following the instructions on the ball band press the garment pieces, omitting the ribs.

Tip: Take special care to press the edges, as this will make sewing up both easier and neater. If the ball band indicates that the fabric is not to be pressed, then covering the blocked out fabric with a damp white cotton cloth and leave it to stand will have the desired effect. Darn in all loose ends neatly along the selvage edge or a colour join, as appropriate.

STITCHING

When stitching the pieces together, remember to match areas of color and texture very carefully where they meet. Use a seam stitch such as backstitch or mattress stitch for all main knitting seams and join all ribs and cuffs with mattress stitch, unless otherwise stated.

TECHNIQUES

HOLDING THE NEEDLES

Not every knitter holds their needles and yarn in the same way. The yarn can be held in either the right or left hand, the needles can be held from above or below. Try each of the methods described here and work in a way that is most comfortable for you. They are all bound to feel awkward and slow at first.

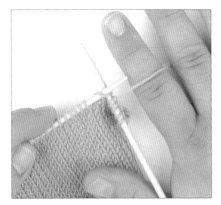

English method
(yarn in the right hand)
Left hand: hold the needle with the stitches in your left hand with your thumb lying along the needle, your index finger resting on top near the tip and the remaining fingers curled under the needle to support it. The thumb and the index finger control the stitches and the tip of the needle.

Right hand: pass the yarn over the index finger, under the middle and over the third finger. The yarn lies between the nail and the first joint and the index finger 'throws' the yarn around the right-hand needle when knitting. The yarn should be able to move freely and is tensioned between the middle and third finger. You can wrap the yarn around the little finger if you feel it is too loose and it keeps falling off your fingers. Hold the empty needle in your right hand with your thumb lying along the needle,

your index finger near the tip and the remaining fingers curled under the needle to support it (see right hand in Continental method).

Some knitters prefer to hold the end of the right-hand needle under their right arm, anchoring it firmly. Whilst knitting this needle remains still and the right hand is above the needle and moves the yarn around it.

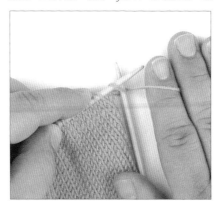

Alternative grip
Left hand: hold the needle in the same way as shown above left.
Right hand: hold the yarn in the fingers the same way as shown above. Hold the needle like a pen, on top of the hand between thumb and index finger. The end of the needle will be above your right arm, in the crook of the elbow. As the fabric grows longer, the thumb will hold the needle behind the knitting

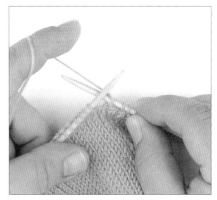

Continental method
(yarn in the left hand)
Left hand: wrap the yarn around your little finger, under the middle two fingers and then over the index finger between the nail and the first joint. The yarn is held taut between the index finger and the needle. Hold the needle with your thumb lying along the needle, your index finger near the tip and remaining fingers curled under the needle to support it. The thumb and index finger control the stitches, yarn and needle tip.

Right hand: hold the empty needle in your right hand with your thumb lying along the needle, index finger resting on top near the tip and remaining fingers curled under the needle to support it. The thumb and index finger control the stitches and the needle tip, which hooks the yarn and draws the loop through.

To begin knitting, you need to work a foundation row of stitches called casting on. There are several ways to cast on depending on the type of edge that you want. The cast on edge should be firm; too loose and it will look untidy and flare out, too tight and it will break and the stitches unravel. If your casting on is always too tight, use a size larger needle. If it is always too loose, use a size smaller needle. Remember to change back to the correct size needle to begin knitting.

Thumb method
This is the simplest way of casting on and you will need only one needle.

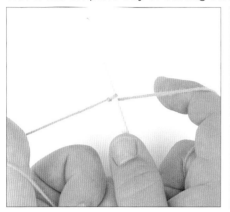
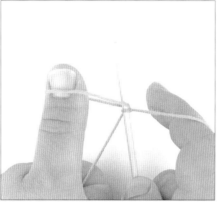
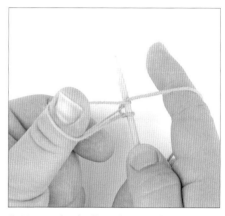

1. Make a slip knot some distance from the end of the yarn (see Knit Perfect) and place it on the needle. Hold the needle in your right hand. Pass the ball end of the yarn over the index finger, under the middle and then over the third finger. Holding the free end of yarn in your left hand, wrap it around your left thumb from front to back.

2. Insert the needle through the thumb loop from front to back.

3. Wrap the ball end over the needle.

The slip knot counts as the first cast on stitch. It is made some distance from the end of the yarn and placed on the needle. Pull the ends of the yarn to tighten it. You now have two ends of yarn coming from the slip knot; the ball end attached to the ball and a shorter free end.

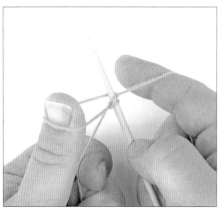

4. Pull a new loop through the thumb loop by passing the thumb loop over the end of the needle. Remove your thumb and tighten the new loop on the needle by pulling the free end. Continue in this way until you have cast on the required number of stitches.

For the thumb method of casting on, you will need approximately 1in (2.5cm) for every stitch you want to cast on. When you have cast on, you should have at least a 6in (15cm) length to sew in.

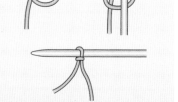

INTRODUCING KNIT STITCH

In knitting there are only two stitches to learn - knit stitch (K) and purl stitch (P). They are the foundation of all knitted fabrics. Once you have mastered these two simple stitches, by combining them in different ways you will soon be knitting ribs, textures, cables and many more exciting fabrics.

English Method (yarn in the right hand)
In knit stitch the yarn is held at the back of the work (the side facing away from you) and is made up of four steps.

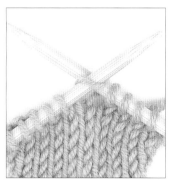 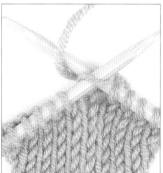  

1. Hold the needle with the cast on stitches in your left hand, and insert the right-hand needle into the front of the stitch from left to right.

2. Pass the yarn under and around the right-hand needle.

3. Pull the new loop on the right-hand needle through the stitch on the left-hand needle.

4. Slip the stitch off the left-hand needle. One knit stitch is completed.

To continue...
Repeat these four steps for each stitch on the left-hand needle. All the stitches on the left-hand needle will be transferred to the right-hand needle where the new row is formed. At the end of the row, swap the needle with the stitches into your left hand and the empty needle into your right hand, and work the next row in the same way.

BINDING (CASTING) OFF

1. Knit two stitches, insert the tip of left-hand needle into the front of the first stitch on the right-hand needle. Lift this stitch over the second stitch and off the needle.

2. One stitch is left on the right-hand needle. Knit the next stitch and lift the second stitch over this and off the needle. Continue in this way until one stitch remains on the right-hand needle.

3. To finish, cut the yarn (leaving a length long enough to sew in), thread the end through the last stitch and slip it off the needle. Pull the yarn end to tighten the stitch and secure.

Bind (cast) off purlwise
To bind (cast) off on a purl row, simply purl the stitches instead of knitting them.

INTRODUCING PURL STITCH

You may find purl stitch a little harder to learn than knit stitch. But really it is just the reverse of a knit stitch. If you purled every row, you would produce garter stitch (the same as if you knitted every row). It is not often that you will work every row in purl stitch; it is easier and faster to knit every row if you want garter stitch.

English method (yarn in the right hand)
In purl stitch the yarn is held at the front of the work (the side facing you) and is made up of four steps.

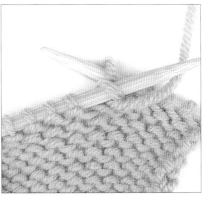

1. Hold the needle with the cast on stitches in your left hand, and insert the right-hand needle into the front of the stitch from right to left.

2. Pass the yarn over and around the right-hand needle.

3. Pull the new loop on the right-hand needle through the stitch on the left-hand needle.

4. Slip the stitch off the left-hand needle. One stitch is completed.

To continue...
Repeat these four steps for each stitch on the left-hand needle. All the stitches on the left-hand needle will be transferred to the right-hand needle where the new purl row is formed. At the end of the row, swap the needle with the stitches into your left hand and the empty needle into your right hand, and work the next row in the same way.

To shape knitting, stitches are increased or decreased. Increases are used to make a piece of knitting wider by adding more stitches, either on the ends of rows or within the knitting.

Some increases are worked to be invisible whilst others are meant to be seen and are known as decorative increases. You can increase one stitch at a time or two or more.

Increasing one stitch

The easiest way to increase one stitch is to work into the front and back of the same stitch. This produces a small bar across the second (increase) satitch and is very visible. This makes counting the increases easier.

On a knit row (Kfb)

1. Knit into the front of the stitch as usual, do not slip the stitch off the left-hand needle but knit into it again through the back of the loop.

2. Slip the original stitch off the left-hand needle. You have now increased an extra stitch and you can see the bar (increased stitch) to the left of the original stitch.

On a purl row (Pfb)

3. Purl into the front of the stitch as usual, do not slip the stitch off the left-hand needle but purl into it again through the back of the loop.

4. Slip the original stitch off the left-hand needle. You have now increased an extra stitch and you can see the bar (increased stitch) to the left of the original stitch.

To make a neater edge when working increases at the beginning and end of rows, work the increase stitches a few stitches from the end. This leaves a continuous stitch up the edge of the fabric that makes sewing up easier. Because the made stitch lies to the left of the original stitch, at the beginning of a knit row you knit one stitch, then make the increase, but at the end of a knit row you work the increase into the third stitch from the end. The increase stitch lies between the second and third stitches at each end.

On a purl row you work in exactly the same way; the bar will be in the correct position two stitches from either end.

This is another way to increase one stitch and is often used where increasing stitches after a rib. The new stitch is made between two existing stitches using the horizontal thread that lies between the stitches - called the running thread. This is an invisible increase and is harder to see when counting.

On a knit row (M1)

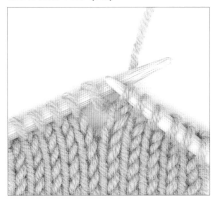

1. Knit to the point where the increase is to be made. Insert the tip of the left-hand needle under the running thread from front to back.

2. Knit this loop through the back to twist it. By twisting the stitch it will prevent leaving a hole appearing where the made stitch is.

On a purl row (M1P)

To work this increase on a purl row, work as given for the knit way but instead purl into the back of the loop.

Increasing more than one stitch

To increase two stitches simply knit into the front, back and then the front again of the same stitch. When knitting bobbles, you will sometimes make five, six or seven stitches out of one stitch in this way. For example, to make seven stitches the instructions would read (k into front and back of same st) 3 times, then k into front again.

Decreasing is used at the ends of rows or within the knitted fabric to reduce the number of stitches being worked on. This means that you can shape your knitted fabric by making it narrower.

Decreasing one stitch

The simplest way to decrease one stitch is to knit or purl two stitches together (K2tog or P2tog). Both of these methods produce the same result on the front (knit side) of the work; the decrease slopes to the right.

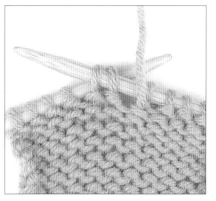

(K2tog or P2tog). Both of these methods produce the same result on the front (knit side) of the work; the decrease slopes to the right.

P2tog on a p row Purl to where the decrease is to be, insert the right-hand needle (as though to purl) through the next two stitches and purl them together as one stitch.

Always read how to work a decrease very carefully. Some of them have similar abbreviations with only a slight difference between them.

In patterns the designer may use different abbreviations to those given here. Always check the detailed explanation of abbreviations.

K2tog tbl on a k row Knit to where the decrease is to be, insert the right-hand needle through the back of the next two stitches and knit them together as one stitch.

P2tog tbl on a p row Purl to where the decrease is to be, insert the right-hand needle through the back of the next two stitches and purl them together as one stitch.

Decorative decreasing one stitch purlwise

Sometimes decreases are decorative, especially in lace knitting where they form part of the pattern. Then you have to be aware of whether the decrease slants right or left. Each decrease has an opposite and the two of them are called a pair. There is one way to work the decrease that is the pair to p2tog which slopes to the left when seen on the front (knit side) of the work.

DECORATIVE DECREASING ONE STITCH KNITWISE

There are two ways to work the decrease that is the pair to K2tog. They both produce the same result and slope to the left.

Slip one, slip one, knit two together (SSK)

1. Slip two stitches knitwise one at a time from left-hand needle to right-hand needle.

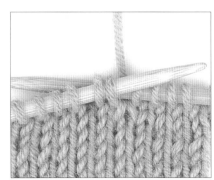

2. Insert the left-hand needle from left to right through the fronts of these two stitches and knit together as one stitch.

Slip one, knit one, pass slipped stitch over (SKPO)

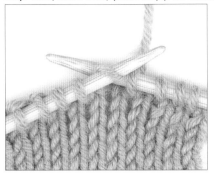

1. Insert the right-hand needle knitwise into the next stitch.

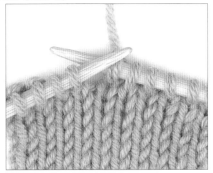

2. Slip it on to the right-hand needle without knitting it, then knit the next stitch.

3. With the tip of the left-hand needle, lift the slipped stitch over the knitted stitch and off the needle. This is like binding (casting) off one stitch.

Slip two, knit one, pass the two slipped stitches over (SK2PO)

1. Insert the right-hand needle knitwise into the next two stitches as if to knit two stitches together without knitting them, slip the two stitches from left-hand needle to right-hand needle.

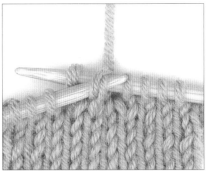

2. Knit the next stitch, then with the tip of left-hand needle, lift the two slipped stitches over the knitted stitch and off the needle.

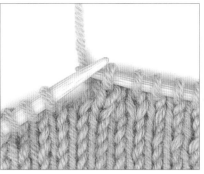

3. You have now completed the central double decrease.

SHORT ROW SHAPING

Short rows are a very popular way to add shaping smoothly and seamlessly and are perfect for making hats. Throughout this book the short row abbreviation is "wrap 1".

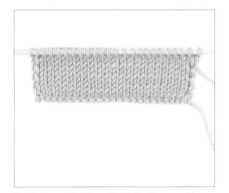

1. Knit as instructed in the pattern until you reach where you will work short rows.

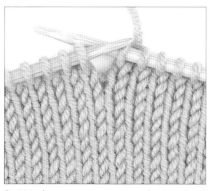

2. Work across a row as instructed until you reach the wrap 1 abbreviation.

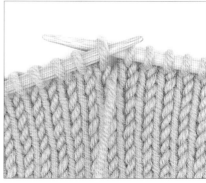

3. Take the yarn between the needles to the opposite side of work. Slip the next stitch purlwise from left needle to right needle, then take yarn back to opposite side of work.

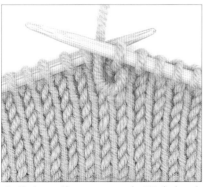

4. Return the wrapped stitch back to left needle.

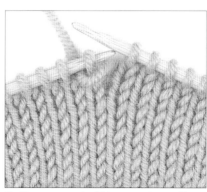

5. Turn your knitting and continue working.

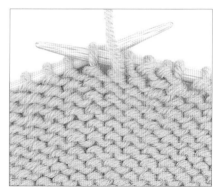

6. Until you reach the next wrap 1 abbreviation.

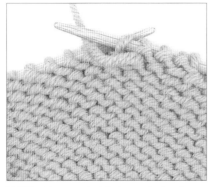

7. Slip the next stitch purlwise from left needle to right needle.

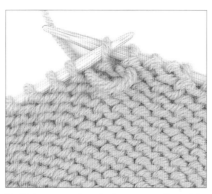

8. Take yarn back to opposite side of work between the needles.

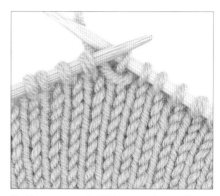

9. Turn your knitting and continue to work as indicated in the pattern.

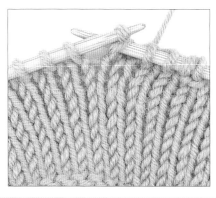

10. When working over a wrapped stitch make sure you work the wrapped stitch with the main stitch together to avoid leaving a line across the right side of your work.

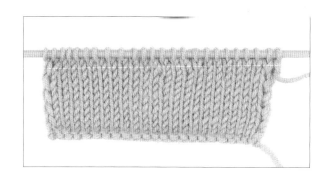

CIRCULAR KNITTING ON DOUBLE-POINTED NEEDLES

Flat knitting is knitted in rows, working back and forth, moving the stitches from one needle to the other. Circular knitting is knitted in rounds, working round and around without turning the work.

working on four needles

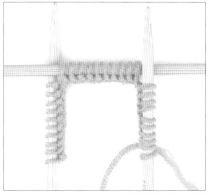

Use a set of four double-pointed needles, adding the stitches at one end and taking them off at the other. Cast the stitches on to one needle and then divide them evenly between three of the needles. For example, if you need to cast on 66 sts, there will be 22 sts on each needle; if you need to cast on 68 sts, there will be 23 sts on two of the needles and 22 on the third. The fourth needle is the working needle.

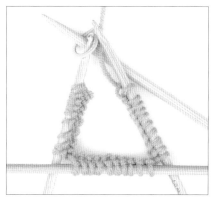

Arrange the needles into a triangle, making sure the cast on edge faces inwards and is not twisted. Place a marker between the last and first cast on stitches to identify the beginning of the round. Slip this marker on every round. Knit the first stitch, pulling up the yarn firmly so there is no gap between the third and first needle. Knit across the rest of the stitches on the first needle. As this needle is now empty, it becomes the working needle.

> The first round is awkward; the needles not being used dangle and get in the way. When you have worked a few rounds the fabric helps hold the needles in shape and knitting will become easier.

> For maximum control, always use the correct length of needle for what you are knitting; short needles for a small number of stitches such as for gloves, and longer needles for garments.

> To avoid a gap at the beginning of the first round, use the tail end of the yarn and the working yarn together to work the first few stitches. Or cast on one extra stitch at the end of the cast on, slip it on to the first needle and knit it together with the first stitch.

> Avoid gaps at the change over between needles by pulling the yarn up tightly, or work a couple of extra stitches from the next needle on each round. This will vary the position of the change over and avoid a ladder of looser stitches forming.

> Double-pointed needles are also used for knitting circles and squares or seamless garments. Use five needles to knit a square, with the stitches divided between the four sides.

Knit the stitches from the second needle, then use the new working needle to knit the stitches from the third needle. One round has been completed. Continue in this way, working in rounds and creating a tube of fabric. By knitting each round you will produce stockinette (stocking) stitch. To produce garter stitch, you will need to knit one round and then purl one round.

GARTER STITCH

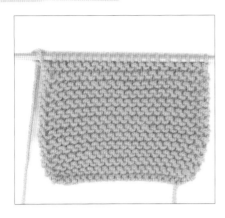

Knit every row

When you knit every row the fabric you make is called garter stitch (g st) and has rows of raised ridges on the front and back of the fabric. It looks the same on the back and the front so it is reversible. Garter stitch lies flat, is quite a thick fabric and does not curl at the edges. These qualities make it ideal for borders and collars, as well as for scarves and the main fabric of a garment.

CABLES

Cable knitting always looks more difficult then it actual is. It is simply done by using a cable needle (third needle) to temporarily hold stitches to be transferred to the front or back of your work. Always remember if the cable needle is at the back of work then the cable will lean to the right. If the cable needle is at the front of work then the cable will lean to the left. There are many different cables, always read the instructions and abbreviations carefully as they may look alike or other designers may use different abbreviations. The number of stitches to be moved will be stated in the pattern. Normally cables are worked only on the right side of work, however I have been known to design garments with cables on the wrong side of work too.

Cable front

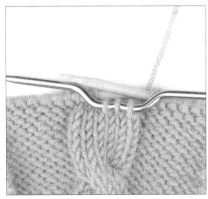

1. Put the number of stitches stated onto a cable needle.

2. Position the cable needle at the front of the work and knit or purl the stated number of stitches from the left-hand needle.

3. Then knit or purl the stated number of stitches from the cable needle.

Cable back

Cable back differs only in that the stitches slipped onto the cable needle are held at the back of the work while the stitches are knitted or purled from the left-hand needle.

Seed (Moss) stitch

Alternate one knit stitch with one purl stitch to the end of the row. On the next row, knit all the purl stitches and purl and the knit stitches as they face you.

1x1 RIB

Alternate one knit stitch with one purl stitch to the end of the row. On the next row, knit all the knit stitches and purl all the purl stitches as they face you.

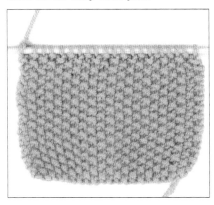

LACE

Simple lace is made up of yarn overs to make a stitch with a pairing decrease to keep the stitch count the same on each row. More complicated lace may have variable stitch counts. No matter which one you are working the rules are the same; If you do not have enough stitches to decrease a yarn over then work this stitch plain and vice versa.

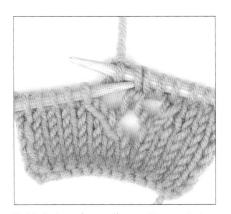
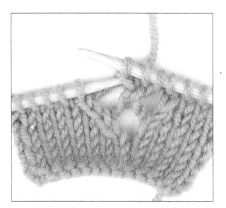
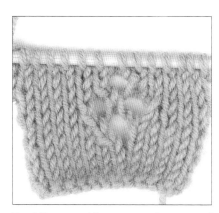

1. Knit to where the pattern states and work a yarn over, by taking the yarn under and over the needle to create a stitch.

2. Work the next two stitches together and work to the end of the row.

3. After working several rows of lace pattern it becomes easier to follow your knitting.

FAIR ISLE

When you knit a design with two or more colors in a design you are constantly switching between them and it is really important to be consistent with the order in which you use them. By this I mean which yarn is stranded "floated" over the top of the other at the back of the work when it is not the color being knitted with at the time.

It is generally accepted that the yarn stranded beneath will be the more dominant colour in the design.

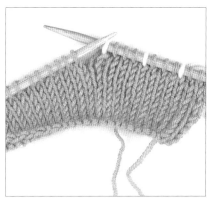

1. Knit to where stated in the pattern. To introduce the new color simply knit the next stitch using the color stated. Pushing the stitches along the right needle as they are worked. This helps to prevent the strands being pulled too tightly between color changes.

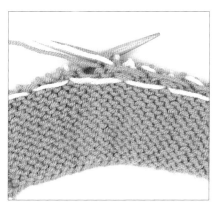

2. Float "strand" the non-working yarn loosely across the back as shown on the wrong side of work.

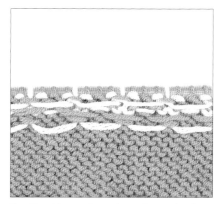

3. Continue to strand as before weaving under and over the working yarn if you are carrying over more than 3 stitches. Continue as set until chart or design is completed.

Here is how your work should look from the right and wrong side.

Right side of work

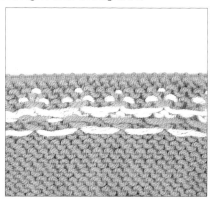

Wrong side of work

MATTRESS STITCH

This technique produces a discreet seam that is especially good if the edge stitches are not very neat, as they become part of the seam inside the project. The other advantage of mattress stitch is that it is worked from the right side of work, so the neatness of the seam can be assessed as the seam is stitched and adjustments made immediately, rather than having to painstakingly unpick the whole seam. Careful preparation will pay dividends, so press and block the pieces first if required, paying particular attention to the edge stitches. Then pin the seams together and matching pattern if there is any to be matched.

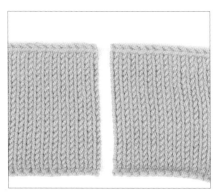

1. Place the edges that need seaming together with right sides of work facing you.

2. Working from the bottom, and between the first and second stitch in from the edge, pass the needle under the loops of two rows on one side; then pass the needle under the loops of the corresponding two rows on other side. Work a few stitches like this before drawing the first stitches tight as this will help to keep track of the line of the seam.

3. The neatest seam is achieved by pulling the yarn just enough to pull the stitches together.

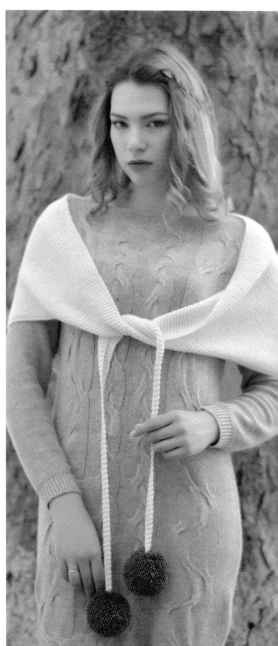

PROJECTS

Frilly Scarf

An open work lace pattern with frills trimmed with pretty picot edging adding flair to the look. This scarf is ideal for summery days.

SIZE
8¼ in (21 cm) wide and 66 in (168 cm) long

ABBREVIATIONS
See inside front flap

MATERIALS NEEDED

DMC Woolly (136 yd/125 m per 50g ball)
6 x Lilac (061)
- US 5 (3.75 mm) needles
- US 6 (4 mm) needles
- 2 Stitch holders

GAUGE (TENSION)
27 sts and 30 rows to 4 in (10 cm) measured over lace patt using US 6 (4 mm) needles.

FRILLS (make 4)

Using US 5 (3.75 mm) needles CO 57 sts.

Row 1 (RS): (K2, Kfb) 18 times, K3. 75 sts.
Beg with a P row, work in st st for 7 rows, ending with RS facing for next row.

Row 9 (picot row) (RS): K1, *yo, K2tog, rep from * to end.
Beg with a P row, work in st st for 7 rows, ending with RS facing for next row.

Row 17 (RS): K tog next st on needle with first st of CO edge, (K to next st on needle with next st of CO edge, K tog next **TWO** sts on needle with next **ONE** st of CO edge, K tog next st on needle with next st of CO edge) 18 times, (K tog next st on needle with next st of CO edge) twice. 57 sts. Cut off yarn and leave sts on a holder.

MAIN SECTION

FIRST HALF

Using US 5 (3.75 mm) needles CO 57 sts.

Row 1 (RS): (K2, Kfb) 18 times, K3. 75 sts
Beg with a P row, work in st st for 9 rows, ending with RS facing for next row.

Row 11 (picot row) (RS): K1, *yo, K2tog, rep from * to end.
Beg with a P row, work in st st for 9 rows, ending with RS facing for next row.

Row 21 (RS): K tog first st on needle with first st of CO edge, (K tog next st on needle with next st of CO edge, K

tog next **TWO** sts on needle with next **ONE** st of CO edge, K tog next st on needle with next st of CO edge) 18 times, (K tog next st on needle with next st of CO edge) twice. 57 sts.

Change to US 6 (4 mm) needles.

Next row (WS): K1, P to last st, K1.

Now work in lace patt as folls:

** **Row 1 (RS):** K1, *K1, yo, K3, skpo, K2tog, K3, yo, rep from * to last st, K1.

Row 2: K1, *yo, P3, P2tog, P2tog tbl, P3, yo, P1, rep from * to last st, K1.

Row 3: K1, *K2, yo, K2, skpo, K2tog, K2, yo, K1, rep from * to last st, K1.

Row 4: K1, *P2, yo, P1, P2tog, P2tog tbl, P1, yo, P3, rep from * to last st, K1.

Row 5: K1, *K4, yo, skpo, K2tog, yo, K3, rep from * to last st, K1.

Row 6: K1, *P4, yo, P2tog, yo, P3, P2tog, rep from * to last st, K1.

Row 7: K1, *K2tog, K3, yo, K1, yo, K3, skpo, rep from * to last st, K1.

Row 8: K1, *P2tog tbl, P3, yo, P1, yo, P3, P2tog, rep from * to last st, K1.

Row 9: K1, *K2tog, K2, yo, K3, yo, K2, skpo, rep from * to last st, K1.

Row 10: K1, *P2tog tbl, P1, yo, P5, yo, P1, P2tog, rep from * to last st, K1.

Row 11: K1, *K2tog, yo, K7, yo, skpo, rep from * to last st, K1.

Row 12: K1, *P2tog, yo, P3, P2tog tbl, P4, yo, rep from * to last st, K1.
These 12 rows form patt.
Cont in patt for a further 23 rows, ending with patt row 11 and **WS** facing for next row.

ATTACH FRILL

Next row (WS): Holding **WS** of frill against RS of sts on needle, P tog first st of frill with first st on left needle, *P tog next st of frill with next st on left needle, rep from * to end. **

Work from ** to ** once more.
Cont straight in lace patt beg with
row 1 until work meas approx 33
in (84 cm), ending with row 6 of
pattern and RS facing for next row.
Cut off yarn and leave sts on a
holder

SECOND HALF

Work exactly as given for first
half, leaving sts on a second
holder and a long tail of yarn.

FINISHING

Graft the 57 sts of first half on
st holder to the 57 sts of second
half on second st holder.
Join row ends of each frill neatly
together on both edges.
Block to measurements carefully
following instructions on ball
band.

2

Snowflake Fair Isle Scarf

Knitted in the round for a seamless finish. This is an updated take and modern mixture of stripes and fair isle. The colors make it ideal for a man, but why not change colors to add a feminine touch.

SIZE

12 in (30 cm) wide and 70 in (178 cm) long

ABBREVIATIONS

See inside front flap

MATERIALS NEEDED

- **DMC Woolly** (136 yd/125 m per 50g ball)
  3 x Light Grey (121) **A**
  5 x Dark Grey (114) **B**
  3 x Teal (077) **C**
  2 x Dark Blue (075) **D**
  2 x Yellow (093 **E**
  1 x Red (052) **F**
- US 5 (3.75 mm) circular needle

GAUGE (TENSION)

25 sts and 28 rounds to 4 in (10 cm) measured over patt using US 5 (3.75 mm) circular needle.

STRIPE SEQUENCE

Rounds 1 and 2: Using yarn **A**.

Rounds 3 and 4: Using yarn **B**.

Rounds 5 and 6: Using yarn **E**.

Rounds 7 and 8: Using yarn **B**.

Rounds 9 and 10: Using yarn **F**.

Rounds 11 and 12: Using yarn **B**.

Rounds 13 and 14: Using yarn **E**.

Rounds 15 and 16: Using yarn **B**.

Rounds 17 and 18: Using yarn **A**.

These 18 rounds form stripe sequence.

SCARF

Using US 5 (3.75 mm) circular needle and yarn **B** CO 144 sts.

Place marker and join for working in the round, being careful not to twist CO edge.

Round 1 (RS): *K2, P2, rep from * to end.
Cut off yarn **B** and join in yarn **A**.
Rep last round 11 times.

Place chart

** Joining in and cutting off colors as required and repeating the 18 st patt repeat 8 times around each round,

çont in patt from chart, which is worked entirely in st st (K every round), until all 31 rounds of chart have been completed.

Beg with round 1, work 18 rounds of stripe sequence (see page 35), which is worked entirely in st st (K every round).

Rep from ** 9 times more, then work 31 rows of chart once more. Change to yarn **A**.

Round 1 (RS): *K2, P2, rep from * to end.
Rep last round 10 times. Cut off yarn **A** and join in yarn **B**. Rep last round once more. BO in rib.

FINISHING

Block to measurements carefully following instructions on ball band. Smooth out the scarf so that it is flat and close the bottom edges together and the top edges together using mattress stitch.

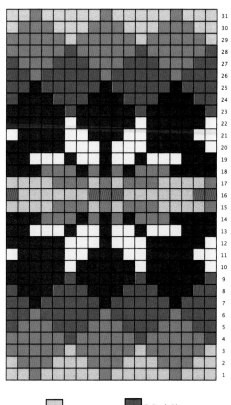

	A Light Grey		D Dark Blue
	B Dark Grey		E Yellow
	C Teal		F Red

3

Chunky Cable and Bobble Scarf

Knitted in a chunky cotton yarn which adds definition to this bold textured pattern in a mixture of twists enhanced by large bobbles.

SIZE
11 in (28 cm) wide and 71½ in (182 cm) long

ABBREVIATIONS
See inside front flap

SPECIAL ABBREVIATIONS

Cr3R slip next st onto CN and leave at back of work, K2, then P1 from CN

Cr3L slip next 2 sts onto CN and leave at front of work, P1, then K2 from CN

C4B slip next 2 sts onto CN and leave at back of work, K2, then K2 from CN

C4F slip next 2 sts onto CN and leave at front of work, K2, then K2 from CN

Cr5R slip next 2 sts onto CN and leave at back of work, K3, then P2 from CN

Cr5L slip next 3 sts onto CN and leave at front of work, P2, then K3 from CN

C6B slip next 3 sts onto CN and leave at back of work, K3, then K3 from CN

MB purl into front, back, then front again of next st, turn, K3, turn, P3, turn, K1, K2tog, turn, P2tog. Push the bobble to RS of work.

MATERIALS NEEDED

- **DMC Natura Just Cotton XL** (82 yd/75 m per 100 g ball) 7 x Wasabi (83)
- US 11 (8 mm) needles
- Cable needle

GAUGE (TENSION)

15 sts and 16 rows to 4 in (10 cm) measured over patt using US 11 (8 mm) needles.

SCARF

Using US 11 (8 mm) needles CO 35 sts.
Row 1 (WS): K2, (Pfb) twice, K5, P2, K5, (Pfb) 3 times, K5, P2, K5, (Pfb) twice, K2. 42 sts.
Now work in patt as folls:

Row 1 (RS): K6, P4, Cr3R, P5, C6B, P5, Cr3L, P4, K6.

Row 2: K2, P4, K4, P2, K6, P6, K6, P2, K4, P4, K2.

Row 3: K2, C4B, P3, Cr3R, P4, Cr5R, Cr5L, P4, Cr3L, P3, C4F, K2.

Row 4: K2, P4, K3, P2, K5, P3, K4, P3, K5, P2, K3, P4, K2.

Row 5: K6, P2, Cr3R, P3, Cr5R, P4, Cr5L, P3, Cr3L, P2, K6.

Row 6: K2, P4, K2, P2, K1, MB, K2, P3, K8, P3, K2, MB, K1, P2, K2, P4, K2.

Row 7: K2, C4B, P2, Cr3L, P3, K3, P8, K3, P3, Cr3R, P2, C4F, K2.

Row 8: K2, P4, K3, P2, K3, P3, K8, P3, K3, P2, K3, P4, K2.

Row 9: K6, P3, Cr3L, P2, Cr5L, P4, Cr5R, P2, Cr3R, P3, K6.

Row 10: K2, P4, K4, P2, (K4, P3) twice, K4, P2, K4, P4, K2.

Row 11: K2, C4B, P4, Cr3L, P3, Cr5L, Cr5R, P3, Cr3R, P4, C4F, K2.

Row 12: K2, P4, K3, MB, K1, P2, K5, P6, K5, P2, K1, MB, K3, P4, K2.
These 12 rows form patt.
Rep these 12 rows 23 times more, then row 1 once more, ending with **WS** facing for next row.

Next row (WS): K2, (P2tog) twice, K4, P2, K6, (P2tog) 3 times, K6, P2, K4, (P2tog) twice, K2. 35 sts.
BO in patt.

FINISHING

Block to measurements carefully following instructions on ball band.

4

Cable Plaited Scarf

A stunning use of cables in a plaited effect emphasis the long lines of this scarf, which adds both warmth and style.

SIZE
8¾ in (22 cm) wide and 79 in (200 cm) long

ABBREVIATIONS
See inside front flap

SPECIAL ABBREVIATION

C12B slip next 6 sts onto CN and leave at back of work, K6, then K6 from CN

C12F slip next 6 sts onto CN and leave at front of work, K6, then K6 from CN

MATERIALS NEEDED

DMC Woolly (136 yd/125 m per 50g ball)
9 x Yellow (093)
- US 6 (4 mm) needles
- Cable needle

GAUGE (TENSION)

39 sts and 34 rows to 4 in (10 cm) measured over cable patt using US 6 (4 mm) needles.

SCARF

Using US 6 (4 mm) needles CO 55 sts.

Next row (WS): K2, (Pfb) 9 times, *K5, (Pfb) 9 times rep from * to last 2 sts, K2. 91 sts.
Cable patt

Row 1 (RS): P2, K18, *P5, K18, rep from * to last 2 sts, P2.

Row 2 and every foll alt row: K2, P18, *K5, P18, rep from * to last 2 sts, K2.

Row 3: P2, K6, C12B, *P5, K6, C12B rep from * to last 2 sts, P2.

Row 5: As row 1.

Row 7: P2, C12F, K6, *P5, C12F, K6 rep from * to last 2 sts, P2.

Row 8: As row 2.
These 8 rows form patt.
Cont in patt until scarf meas approx 79 in (200 cm), ending with row 1 of patt and **WS** facing for next row.

Next row (WS): K2, (P2tog) 9 times, *K5, (P2tog) 9 times rep from * to last 2 sts, K2. 55 sts.
BO in patt.

FINISHING

Block to measurements carefully following instructions on ball band.

5

Checker Fair Isle Cowl

Alternating blocks of solid color and fair isle in this simple two color cowl.
The double rib at the top and bottom allow for an easy fit and comfort.

SIZE
25 in (65 cm) circumference and 12 ½ in (32 cm) wide

ABBREVIATIONS
See inside front flap

MATERIALS NEEDED

DMC Woolly (136 yd/125 m per 50g ball)
2 x Brown (116) **A**
1 x Orange (010) **B**
• US 5 (3.75 mm) circular needle

GAUGE (TENSION)
23.5 sts and 28 rounds to 4 in (10 cm) measured over patt using US 5 (3.75 mm) circular needle.

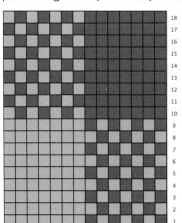

Key

A Brown

B Orange

COWL

Using US 5 (3.75 mm) circular needle and yarn **A** CO 168 sts.
Place marker and join for working in the round, being careful not to twist CO edge.

Round 1 (RS): *K2, P2, rep from * to end.
Rep last round 7 times more.

Place chart

** Joining in and cutting off colors as required and repeating the 14 st patt repeat 12 times around each round, cont in patt from chart, which is worked entirely in st st (K every round), until all 18 rounds of chart have been completed.
Rep from ** once more, then work rounds 1 to 9 of chart once more.
Change to yarn **A**.

Round 54: Knit.

Round 55 (RS): *K2, P2, rep from * to end.
Rep last round 7 times.
BO in rib.

FINISHING

Block to measurements carefully following instructions on ball band.

6

Easy Cable Scarf

Fine cable detail with rows of rib separating them gives a manly and simple look.

SIZE

8 in (20 cm) wide, 59 ¼ in (150 cm) long

ABBREVIATIONS

See inside front flap

SPECIAL ABBREVIATION

C4F slip next 2 sts onto CN and leave at front of work, K2, then K2 from CN

MATERIALS NEEDED

DMC Woolly (136 yd/125 m per 50g ball)
6 x Dark Blue (075)
- US 5 (3.75 mm) needles
- Cable needle

GAUGE (TENSION)

30 sts and 30 rows to 4 in (10 cm) measured over patt and slightly stretched using US 5 (3.75 mm) needles.

SCARF

Using US 5 (3.75 mm) needles CO 60 sts.

Row 1 (RS): K3, P2, *K2, P2, rep from * to last 3 sts, K3.

Row 2: K1, P2, *K2, P2, rep from * to last st, K1.
Last 2 rows form rib.
Work a further 11 rows, ending with **WS** facing for next row.

Next row (WS): K1, *P2, K2, (Pfb) twice, K2, rep from * to last 3 sts, P2, K1. 74 sts.

Now work in cable patt as folls:

Row 1 (RS): K3, *P2, K4, P2, K2, rep from * to last st, K1.

Row 2: K1, *P2, K2, P4, K2, rep from * to last 3 sts, P2, K1.

Row 3: K3, *P2, C4F, P2, K2, rep from * to last st, K1.

Row 4: As row 2.
These 4 rows form patt.
Cont in patt until scarf meas 57 in (145 cm), ending with row 1 of patt and **WS** facing for next row.

Next row (WS): K1, *P2, K2, (P2tog) twice, K2, rep from * to last 3 sts, P2, K1. 60 sts.

Row 1 (RS): K3, P2, *K2, P2, rep from * to last 3 sts, K3.

Row 2: K1, P2, *K2, P2, rep from * to last st, K1.
Last 2 rows form rib.
Work a further 10 rows, ending with RS facing for next row.
BO in rib.

FINISHING

Block to measurements carefully following instructions on ball band.

Easy Striped Scarf

Worked in two halves this tonal stocking stitch scarf naturally rolls up giving a sleek and fresh look.

SIZE
8 ½ in (22 cm) wide and 59 in (150 cm) long

ABBREVIATIONS
See inside front flap

MATERIALS NEEDED

DMC Woolly (136 yd/125 m per 50g ball)
2 x Teal Blue (077) **A**
2 x Duck Egg (073) **B**
- US 5 (3.75 mm) needles
- US 6 (4 mm) needles
- Stitch holders

GAUGE (TENSION)

22 sts and 30 rows to 4 in (10 cm) measured over st st using US 6 (4 mm) needles.

STRIPE SEQUENCE

Rows 1 and 2: Using yarn **B**.

Rows 3 and 4: Using yarn **A**.

Rows 5 and 6: Using yarn **B**.

Rows 7 and 8: Using yarn **A**.

Rows 9 and 10: Using yarn **B**.

Rows 11 to 18: Using yarn **A**.

Rows 19 and 20: Using yarn **B**.

Rows 21 to 24: Using yarn **A**.

Rows 25 and 26: Using yarn **B**.

Rows 27 to 30: Using yarn **A**.

Rows 31 and 32: Using yarn **B**.

Rows 33 to 40: Using yarn **A**.
These 40 rows form stripe sequence and are repeated.

SCARF

FIRST HALF

Using US 5 (3.75 mm) needles and yarn **A** CO 52 sts.

Row 1 (RS): K4, *P4, K4, rep from * to end.

Row 2: P4, *K4, P4, rep from * to end. Last 2 rows form rib. Work a further 12 rows in rib, ending with RS facing for next row. Change to US 6 (4 mm) needles. Beg with row 1, work in stripe sequence (see left column), which is worked entirely in st st beg with a K row. Cont in stripe sequence repeating the 40 rows 5 times more, ending with RS facing for next row. Leave these sts on a holder.

SECOND HALF

Work as given for first half, but working yarn **A** as yarn **B** and yarn **B** as yarn **A** throughout.

FINISHING

With RS of both halves together and WS outside, BO both sets of 52 sts together.
Block to measurements carefully following instructions on ball band.

8

Aran Style Scarf

A twisted cable frames the honeycomb pattern, giving a touch of tradition aran a modern edge.

SIZE

8¼ in (21 cm) wide and 79 in (200 cm) long

ABBREVIATIONS

See inside front flap

SPECIAL ABBREVIATIONS

C4B slip next 2 sts onto CN and leave at back of work, K2, then K2 fromw CN

C4F slip next 2 sts onto CN and leave at front of work, K2, then K2 from CN

C6B slip next 3 sts onto CN and leave at back of work, K3, then K3 from CN

C6F slip next 2 sts onto CN and leave at front of work, K3, then K3 from CN

MATERIALS NEEDED

DMC Woolly (136 yd/125 m per 50g ball)
7 x Cream (003)
- US 5 (3.75 mm) needles
- US 6 (4 mm) needles
- Cable needle

GAUGE (TENSION)

26.5 sts and 28 rows to 4 in (10 cm) measured over patt using US 6 (4 mm) needles.

SCARF

Using US 5 (3.75 mm) needles CO 56 sts.

Row 1 (RS): K1, *K2, P2, rep from * to last 3 sts, K3.

Row 2: K1, *P2, K2, rep from * to last 3 sts, P2, K1.
Last 2 rows form rib.
Cont in rib for a further 15 rows, ending with **WS** facing for next row.

Next row (WS): K2, Pfb, P2, Pfb, K1, Pfb, P2, Pfb, K2, (P1, Pfb, P1) 10 times, K2, Pfb, P2, Pfb, K1, Pfb, P2, Pfb, K2. 74 sts.

Change to US 6 (4 mm) needles.

Now work in cable patt as folls:

Row 1 (RS): K2, C6F, P1, C6B, P2, (C4B, C4F) 5 times, P2, C6F, P1, C6B, K2.

Row 2 and every foll alt row: K2, P6, K1, P6, K2, P40, K2, P6, K1, P6, K2.

Row 3: K8, P1, K6, P2, K40, P2, K6, P1, K8.

Row 5: K8, P1, K6, P2, (C4F, C4B) 5 times, P2, K6, P1, K8.

Row 7: As row 3.

Row 8: As row 2. Last 8 rows form patt.
Cont in patt until scarf meas approx 76½ in (194 cm), ending with patt row 5 and **WS** facing for next row.

Change to US 5 (3.75 mm) needles.

Next row (WS): K2, P2tog, P2, P2tog, K1, P2tog, P2, P2tog, K2, (P1, P2tog, P1) 10 times, K2, P2tog, P2, P2tog, K1, P2tog, P2, P2tog, K2. 56 sts.

Row 1 (RS): K1, *K2, P2, rep from * to last 3 sts, K3.

Row 2: K1, *P2, K2, rep from * to last 3 sts, P2, K1.
Last 2 rows form rib.

Cont in rib for a further 15 rows, ending with **WS** facing for next row.
BO in patt (on **WS**).

FINISHING

Block to measurements carefully following instructions on ball band.

9

Cabled Snood

This longer style cowl is packed with stitch detail.
Twists, diamonds and bobbles are all in the mix.

SIZE

10 in (25 cm) wide and 47¼ in (120 cm) long

ABBREVIATIONS

See inside front flap

SPECIAL ABBREVIATION

C3B slip next st onto CN and leave at back of work, K2, then K1 from CN

C3F slip next 2 sts onto CN and leave at front of work, K1, then K2 from CN

Cr3R slip next st onto CN and leave at back of work, K2, then P1 from CN

Cr3L slip next 2 sts onto CN and leave at front of work, P1, then K2 from CN

C6B slip next 3 sts onto CN and leave at back of work, K3, then K3 from CN

C6F slip next 3 sts onto CN and leave at front of work, K3, then K3 from CN

MB knit into front and back then front of next st, turn, P3, turn, K3, turn, P1, P2tog, turn, K2tog.

MATERIALS NEEDED

DMC Woolly (136 yd/125 m per 50g ball)
6 x Lime Green (084)
- US 6 (4 mm) needles
- Cable needle

GAUGE (TENSION)

28 sts and 36 rows to 4 in (10 cm) measured over patt using US 6 (4 mm) needles.

SNOOD

Using US 6 (4 mm) needles and waste yarn CO 70 sts.

Row 1 (RS): K1, P1, K1, P2, K1, P1, *K7, P1, K1, P1, K3, P1, (K1, P1) twice, K3, P2, K1, P1, rep from * once more, K7, (P1, K1) 3 times.

Row 2: K1, P1, K3, P1, K1, *P7, K1, P1, K1, P1 (P1, K1) 4 times, P2, K2, P1, K1, rep from * once more, P7, K1, P1, K2, P1, K1.

Change to main yarn and work as folls:
Beg and ending rows as indicated, repeating chart rows 1 to 20 throughout, 22 times in total, snood should meas approx 47¼ in (120 cm) from first row in main yarn and ending with RS facing for next row.

Cut off yarn, leaving a fairly long end.

FINISHING

Join center back seam of Snood by grafting together sts of last row and sts of first row in main yarn, unravelling waste yarn from CO edge at same time.

Block to measurements carefully following instructions on ball band.

Key

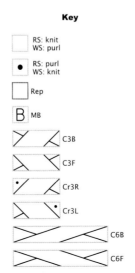

RS: knit WS: purl	
•	RS: purl WS: knit
	Rep
B	MB
⟋ ⟍	C3B
⟍ ⟍	C3F
⟋ ⟍	Cr3R
⟍ ⟍	Cr3L
⟋⟍	C6B
⟋⟍	C6F

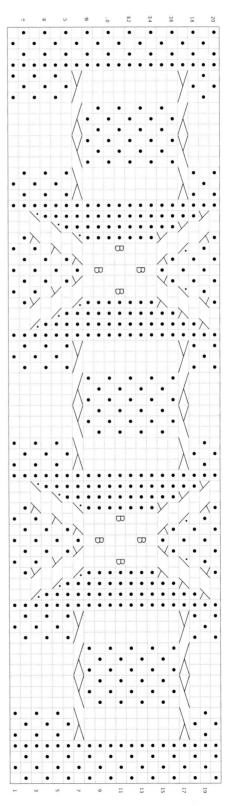

10

Leaf Edged Scarf

Delicate shaped leaves edge this garter stitch scarf.
The simplicity of the design is enhanced by the individual knitted leaves.

SIZE
10 in (25 cm) wide and 71 in (180 cm) long

ABBREVIATIONS
See inside front flap

SPECIAL ABBREVIATIONS
sm slip marker
sl 2 slip the next 2 sts together as though to K2tog without knitting them

MATERIALS NEEDED

DMC Woolly (136 yd/125 m per 50g ball)
6 x Dark Lime (081)
• US 6 (4 mm) needles
• Cable needle

GAUGE (TENSION)

22 sts and 42 rows to 4 in (10 cm) measured over g st using US 6 (4 mm) needles.

SCARF

Using US 6 (4 mm) needles CO 42 sts, counting in from either end, placing a marker between the 6th and 7th st.

Row 1 (RS): K2, yo, K1, yo, K3, sm, K30, sm, K3, yo, K1, yo, K2. 46 sts.

Row 2: P6, Kfb, K1, sm, K30, sm, K1, Kfb, P6. 48 sts.

Row 3: K3, yo, K1, yo, K2, P1, K2, sm, K30, sm, K2, P1, K2, yo, K1, yo, K3. 52 sts.

Row 4: P8, Kfb, K2, sm, K30, sm, K2, Kfb, P8. 54 sts.

Row 5: K4, yo, K1, yo, K3, P2, K2, sm, K30, sm, K2, P2, K3, yo, K1, yo, K4. 58 sts.

Row 6: P10, Kfb, K3, sm, K30, sm, K3, Kfb, P10. 60 sts.

Row 7: K1, skpo, K5, K2tog, P3, K2, sm, K30, sm, K2, P3, skpo, K5, K2tog, K1. 56 sts.

Row 8: P8, Kfb, P1, K3, sm, K30, sm, K3, P1, Kfb, P8. 58 sts.

Row 9: K1, skpo, K3, K2tog, P2, K1, P1, K2, sm, K30, sm, K2, P1,K1, P2, skpo, K3, K2tog, K1. 54 sts.

Row 10: P6, Kfb, K1, P1, K3, sm, K30, sm, K3, P1, K1, Kfb, P6. 56 sts.

Row 11: K1, skpo, K1, K2tog, P3, K1, P1, K2, sm, K30, sm, K2, P1, K1, P3, skpo, K1, K2tog, K1. 52 sts.

Row 12: P4, Kfb, K2, P1, K3, sm, K30, sm, K3, P1, K2, Kfb, P4. 54 sts.

Row 13: K1, sl 2, K1, psso, P4, K1, P1, K2, sm, K30, sm, K2, P1, K1, P4, sl 2, K1, psso, K1. 50 sts.

Row 14: P2tog, BO 3 sts knitwise (1 st on right needle after BO), K1, P1, K3, sm, K30, sm, K3, P1, K4, P2. 46 sts.

Row 15: Skpo, BO 3 sts purlwise (1 st on right needle after BO), P1, K1, P1, K2, sm, K30, sm, K2, P1, K1, P2. 42 sts.

Row 16: K2, P1, K3, sm, K30, sm, K3, P1, K2. 42 sts.

Rep the last 16 rows 46 times more, Scarf should meas approx 71 in (180 cm), ending with row 16 of patt and RS facing for next row.

BO in patt.

FINISHING

Block to measurements carefully following instructions on ball band.

11

Flower Scarf

A picturesque floral scarf in two contrasting colors with intricate floral and leaf detail. The light and dark tones highlight the beauty of this pattern.

SIZE

14 in (36 cm) wide and 71¼ in (181 cm) long

ABBREVIATIONS

See inside front flap

MATERIALS NEEDED

DMC Woolly (136 yd/125 m per 50g ball)
10 x Purple (065) **A**
8 x Magenta (063) **B**
•   US 5 (3.75 mm) circular needle

GAUGE (TENSION)

25 sts and 28 rounds to 4 in (10 cm) measured over patt using US 5 (3.75 mm) circular needle.

STRIPE SEQUENCE

Rounds 1 and 2: Using yarn **A**.

Rounds 3 and 4: Using yarn **B**   .

Rounds 5 and 6: Using yarn **A**.
These 6 rounds form stripe sequence.

SCARF

Using US 5 (3.75 mm) circular needle and yarn **A** CO 180 sts.

Place marker and join for working in the round, being careful not to twist CO edge.
Beg with round 1, work 6 rounds of stripe sequence (see left column), which is worked entirely in st st (K every round), increasing 2 sts evenly across last round. 182 sts.

PLACE CHART A

Joining in and cutting off colors as required and repeating the 91 st patt repeat twice around each round, cont in patt from chart, which is worked entirely in st st (K every round), until all 89 rounds of chart have been completed.

Beg with round 1, work 6 rounds of stripe sequence (see left column), which is worked entirely in st st (K every round), decreasing 2 sts evenly across last round. 180 sts.

PLACE CHART B

Joining in and cutting off colors as required and repeating the 20 st patt repeat 9 times around each round, cont in patt from chart, which is worked entirely in st st (K every round), until you have repeated the 18 rounds of chart 17 times in total.

Beg with round 1, work 6 rounds of stripe sequence (see page 65), which is worked entirely in st st (K every round), increasing 2 sts evenly across last round. 182 sts.

PLACE CHART A

Joining in and cutting off colors as required and repeating the 91 st patt repeat twice around each round, cont in patt from chart, which is worked entirely in st st (K every round), until all 89 rounds of chart have been completed.

Beg with round 1, work 6 rounds of stripe sequence (see page 65), which is worked entirely in st st (K every round), decreasing 2 sts evenly across last round. 180 sts.

BO using yarn **A**.

FINISHING

Block to measurements carefully following instructions on ball band. Smooth out the scarf so that it is flat and close the bottom edges together and the top edges together using mattress stitch.

Chart A

Chart B

A Purple

B Magenta

12

Braided Cable Scarf

This scarf has impact with its bold and spaced braided cables set on a reverse stocking stitch background.

SIZE
6 ¼ in (16 cm) wide and 98½ in (250 cm) long

ABBREVIATIONS
See inside front flap

SPECIAL ABBREVIATION

C8B slip next 4 sts onto CN and leave at back of work, K4, then K4 from CN

C8F slip next 4 sts onto CN and leave at front of work, K4, then K4 from CN

C24B slip next 12 sts onto CN and leave at back of work, slip next 4 sts onto second CN and leave at front of work, K4, then K4 from second CN, K4, slip all the sts from rem CN back onto left needle, slip next 4 sts onto CN and leave at front of work, K4, then K4 from CN, K4

MATERIALS NEEDED

DMC Woolly (136 yd/125 m per 50g ball)
 8 x Pink (042)
 • US 6 (4 mm) needles
 • 2 x Cable needles

GAUGE (TENSION)

33 sts and 34 rows to 4 in (10 cm) measured over cable patt using US 6 (4 mm) needles.

SCARF

Using US 6 (4 mm) needles CO 42 sts.

Next row (RS): K1, (Kfb) 6 times, P5, (Kfb) 6 times, P6, (Kfb) 6 times, P5, (Kfb) 6 times, K1. 66 sts.

Cable patt

Row 1 (WS): K1, P12, K5, P12, K6, P12, K5, P12, K1.

Row 2: K5, C8B, P5, M1P, K4, C8B, P2tog, P2, P2tog tbl, K4, C8B, M1P, P5, K4, C8B, K1.

Row 3: K1, P12, K6, P12, K4, P12, K6, P12, K1.

Row 4: K13, P6, K12, P4, K12, P6, K13.

Row 5: As row 3.

Row 6: K1, C8F, K4, P6, M1P, C8F, K4, P2tog, P2tog tbl, C8F, K4, M1P, P6, C8F, K5.

Row 7: K1, P12, K7, P12, K2, P12, K7, P12, K1.

Row 8: K13, P7, K12, P2, K12, P7, K13.

Row 9: As row 7.

Row 10: K5, C8B, P7, M1P, K4, C8B, K3tog, K3, C8B, M1P, P7, K4, C8B, K1.

Row 11: K1, P12, K8, P24, K8, P12, K1.

Row 12: K13, P8, K24, P8, K13.

Row 13: As row 11.

Row 14: K1, C8F, K4, P8, C24B, P8, C8F, K5.

Rows 15 and 16: As rows 11 and 12.

Row 17: As row 11.

Row 18: K5, C8B, P6, P2tog tbl, K4, C8B, (P1, P1 tbl, K1) all into next st, K3, C8B, P2tog, P6, K4, C8B, K1.

Rows 19 and 20: As rows 7 and 8.

Row 21: As row 7.

Row 22: K1, C8F, K4, P5, P2tog tbl, C8F, K4, M1P, P2, M1P, C8F, K4, P2tog, P5, C8F, K5.

Rows 23 and 24: As rows 3 and 4.

Row 25: As row 3.

Row 26: K5, C8B, P4, P2tog tbl, K4, C8B, M1P, P4, M1P, K4, C8B, P2tog, P4, K4, C8B, K1.

Row 27: As row 1.

Row 28: K13, P5, K12, P6, K12, P5, K13.

Row 29: As row 1.

Row 30: K1, C8F, K4, P3, P2tog tbl, C8F, K4, M1P, P6, M1P, C8F, K4, P2tog, P3, C8F, K5.

Row 31: K1, P12, K4, P12, K8, P12, K4, P12, K1.

Row 32: K13, P4, K12, P8, K12, P4, K13.

Row 33: As row 31.

Row 34: K5, C8B, P2, P2tog tbl, K4, C8B, M1P, P8, M1P, K4, C8B, P2tog, P2, K4, C8B, K1.

Row 35: K1, P12, K3, P12, K10, P12, K3, P12, K1.

Row 36: K13, P3, K12, P10, K12, P3, K13.

Row 37: As row 35.

Row 38: K1, C8F, K4, P1, P2tog tbl, C8F, K4, M1P, P10, M1P, C8F, K4, P2tog, P1, C8F, K5.

Row 39: K1, P12, K2, P12, K12, P12, K2, P12, K1.

Row 40: K13, P2, K12, P12, K12, P2, K13.

Row 41: As row 39.

Row 42: K5, C8B, P2, K4, C8B, P12, K4, C8B, P2, K4, C8B, K1.

Rows 43 and 44: As rows 39 and 40.

Row 45: As row 39.

Row 46: K1, C8F, K4, P2, M1P, C8F, K4, P2tog, P8, P2tog tbl, C8F, K4, M1P, P2, C8F, K5.

Rows 47 and 48: As rows 35 and 36.

Row 49: As row 35.

Row 50: K5, C8B, P3, M1P, K4, C8B, P2tog, P6, P2tog tbl, K4, C8B, M1P, P3, K4, C8B, K1.

Rows 51 and 52: As rows 31 and 32.

Row 53: As row 31.

Row 54: K1, C8F, K4, P4, M1P, C8F, K4, P2tog, P4, P2tog tbl, C8F, K4, M1P, P4, C8F, K5.

Row 55: As row 1.

Row 56: As row 28.

Last 56 rows form patt.
Cont in patt until work meas approx 98½ in (250 cm), ending with row 26 and **WS** facing for next row.

Next row (WS): K1, (P2tog) 6 times, K5, (P2tog) 6 times, K6, (P2tog) 6 times, K5, (P2tog) 6 times, K1. 42 sts.
BO in patt.

FINISHING

Block to measurements carefully following instructions on ball band.

13

Simple 3x3 Rib Cowl

Knitted in a broad rib this cowl is quick and easy to make and is ideal for using up yarn as it only takes 3 balls. The rib allows for stretch, comfort ad warmth.

SIZE
10 in (25 cm) deep and 28 in (71 cm) circumference

ABBREVIATIONS
See inside front flap

SPECIAL ABBREVIATION
wyab with yarn at back

MATERIALS NEEDED
DMC Woolly (136 yd/125 m per 50g ball)
3 x Pink (043)
• US 6 (4 mm) circular needle

GAUGE (TENSION)
26 sts and 32 rows to 4 in (10 cm) measured over patt slightly stretched using US 6 (4 mm) needles.

COWL
Using US 6 (4 mm) circular needle CO 198 sts.
Place marker and join for working in the round, being careful not to twist CO edge.

Round 1 (RS): *K3, P3, rep from * to end.

Round 2: *K1, wyab sl 1 purlwise, K1, P3, rep from * to end.
Last 2 rounds forms patt.
Cont in patt until work meas approx 10 in (25 cm), ending with round 1.

BO row: *K2tog (1 st on right needle), slip this st back onto left needle, rep from * until 1 st rem then fasten off.

FINISHING
Block to measurements carefully following instructions on ball band.

14

Two Color
Garter Stitch Scarf

*Knitted in chunky crisp cotton which defines the simplicity of the stitches.
This two color block design is perfect for the beginner or a quick knit for
the skilled.*

SIZE

8½ in (22 cm) wide and 86½ in (220 cm) long

ABBREVIATIONS

See inside front flap

MATERIALS NEEDED

DMC Natura Just Cotton XL (82 yd/75 m per 100g
ball)
1 x Emeraude (81) **A**
5 x Ecru (03) **B**
• US 10 (6 mm) needles

GAUGE (TENSION)

13 sts and 26 rows to 4 in (10 cm) measured over g st
using US 10 (6 mm) needles.

SCARF

Using US 10 (6 mm) needles and yarn **A** CO 28 sts.
Work in g st for 30 rows, ending with RS facing for next
row.
Change to yarn **B**.
Work in g st until work meas 81 in (206 cm), ending
with RS facing for next row.
Change to yarn **A**.
Work in g st for 31 rows, ending with **WS** facing for next
row.
BO knitwise (on **WS**).

FINISHING

Cover with a damp cloth and leave to dry naturally.

15

Celtic Cable Scarf

Diamond and lattice work is two key features of this richly textured knit. The twisted cable gives the edges of the diamonds a firm neat finish.

SIZE

5 in (15 cm) wide and 86½ in (220 cm) long

ABBREVIATIONS

See inside front flap

SPECIAL ABBREVIATION

C2B slip next st onto CN and leave at back of work, K1, then K1 from CN

C2F slip next st onto CN and leave at front of work, K1, then K1 from CN

C5B slip next 2 sts onto CN and leave at back of work, K3, then K2 from CN

C5F slip next 3 sts onto CN and leave at front of work, K2, then K3 from CN

Cr5R slip next 2 sts onto CN and leave at back of work, K3, then P2 from CN

Cr5L slip next 3 sts onto CN and leave at front of work, P2, then K3 from CN

C6B slip next 3 sts onto CN and leave at back of work, K3, then K3 from CN

C6F slip next 3 sts onto CN and leave at front of work, K3, then K3 from CN

MATERIALS NEEDED

DMC Woolly (136 yd/125 m per 50g ball)
7 x Lime (084)
- US 6 (4 mm) needles
- Cable needle

GAUGE (TENSION)

35 sts and 34 rows to 4 in (10 cm) measured over cable patt using US 6 (4 mm) needles.

SCARF

Using US 6 (4 mm) needles CO 47 sts.

Next row (WS): K1, (Pfb) 3 times, P3, K2, Pfb, P1, *K4, (Pfb) 3 times, rep from * twice more, K4, P1, Pfb, K2, P3, (Pfb) 3 times, K1. 64 sts.

Cable patt

Row 1 (RS): K1, C6B, K3, P2, K3, (P4, C6F) 3 times, P4, K3, P2, K3, C6F, K1.

Row 2: K1, P9, K2, P3, (K4, P6) 3 times, K4, P3, K2, P9, K1.

Row 3: K4, C6F, P2, (Cr5L, Cr5R) 4 times, P2, C6B, K4.

Row 4: K1, P9, (K4, P6) 4 times, K4, P9, K1.

Row 5: K1, C6B, K3, (P4, C6B) 4 times, P4, K3, C6F, K1.

Row 6: As row 4.

Row 7: K4, C6F, P2, (Cr5R, Cr5L) 4 times, P2, C6B, K4.

Rows 8 and 9: As rows 2 and 1.

Rows 10 and 11: As rows 2 and 3.

Row 12: K1, P9, (K4, P6) twice, K1, P2, K1, (P6, K4) twice, P9, K1.

Row 13: K1, C6B, K3, P4, C6B, P4, K1, Cr5R, P1, C2B, P1, Cr5L, K1, P4, C6B, P4, K3, C6F, K1.

Row 14: K1, P9, K4, P6, K4, P4, K3, P2, K3, P4, K4, P6, K4, P9, K1.

Row 15: K4, C6F, P2, Cr5R, K3, P3, C5B, P2, C2B, C2F, P2, C5F, P3, K3, Cr5L, P2, C6B, K4.

Row 16: K1, P9, (K2, P3) twice, K3, P5, (K2, P1) twice, K2, P5, K3, (P3, K2) twice, P9, K1.

Row 17: K1, C6B, K3, P2, K3, Cr5R, P1, Cr5R, C2B, P1, C2B, K2, C2F, P1, C2F, Cr5L, P1, Cr5L, K3, P2, K3, C6F, K1.

Row 18: K1, P9, K2, P6, K3, P3, K2, P2, K1, P2, K2, P2, K1, P2, K2, P3, K3, P6, K2, P9, K1.

Row 19: K4, C6F, P2, C6B, P1, Cr5R, P2, C2B, P1, C2B, K2, C2F, P1, C2F, P2, Cr5L, P1, C6F, P2, C6B, K4.

Row 20: K1, P9, K2, P6, K1, P3, K4, P2, (K2, P1) twice, K2, P2, K4, P3, K1, P6, K2, P9, K1.

Row 21: K1, C6B, K3, P2, K6, P1, K3, P4, C2B, P2, K4, P2, C2F, P4, K3, P1, K6, P2, K3, C6F, K1.

Row 22: As row 20.

Row 23: K4, C6F, P2, C6B, P1, Cr5L, P2, C2B, P1, C2F, K2, C2B, P1, C2F, P2, Cr5R, P1, C6F, P2, C6B, K4.

Row 24: K1, P9, K2, P6, K3, P3, K2, P2, K1, P2, K2, P2, K1, P2, K2, P3, K3, P6, K2, P9, K1.

Row 25: K1, C6B, K3, P2, K3, Cr5L, P1, Cr5L, C2B, P1, C2F, K2, C2B, P1, C2F, Cr5R, P1, Cr5R, K3, P2, K3, C6F, K1.

Row 26: K1, P9, (K2, P3) twice, K3, P5, (K2, P1) twice, K2, P5, K3, (P3, K2) twice, P9, K1.

Row 27: K4, C6F, P2, Cr5L, K3, P3, C5F, P2, C2F, C2B, P2, C5B, P3, K3, Cr5R, P2, C6B, K4.

Row 28: K1, P9, (K4, P6) twice, K1, P2, K1, (P6, K4) twice, P9, K1.

Row 29: K1, C6B, K3, P4, C6B, P4, C6F, P1, C2B, P1, (C6B, P4) twice, K3, C6F, K1.

Rows 30 and 31: As rows 28 and 7.

Rows 32 and 33: As rows 2 and 1.

Rows 34 and 35: As rows 2 and 3.

Rows 36 and 37: As rows 4 and 5.

Rows 38 and 39: As rows 4 and 7.

Row 40: As row 2.

These 40 rows form patt.
Cont in patt until scarf meas approx 86½ in (220 cm), ending with row 1 of patt and **WS** facing for next row.

Next row (WS): K1, (P2tog) 3 times, P3, K2, P2tog, P1, *K4, (P2tog) 3 times, rep from * twice more, K4, P1, P2tog, K2, P3, (P2tog) 3 times, K1. 64 sts.
BO in patt.

FINISHING

Block to measurements carefully following instructions on ball band.

16

Diamond Cabled Cowl

This trellis effect diamond design is on a background of alternate rows of moss and stocking stitch, with garter stitch rows bordering the top and bottom.

SIZE
7½ in (18 cm) deep and 25 in (64 cm) circumference

ABBREVIATIONS
See inside front flap

SPECIAL ABBREVIATION

C4R slip next st onto CN and leave at back of work, K3, then K1 from CN

C4L slip next 3 sts onto CN and leave at front of work, K1, then K3 from CN

MATERIALS NEEDED

DMC Woolly (136 yd/125 m per 50g ball)
2 x Blue (072)
- US 6 (4 mm) circular needle
- Cable needle

GAUGE (TENSION)

22 sts and 36 rows to 4 in (10 cm) measured over cable patt using US 6 (4 mm) needles.

COWL

Using US 6 (4 mm) circular needle CO 140 sts.
Place marker and join for working in the round, being careful not to twist CO edge.

Round 1 (RS): Knit to marker.

Round 2: Purl to marker.
Rep last 2 rounds twice more.

Next round: *(Kfb) twice, K6, (Kfb) twice, rep from * to marker. 196 sts.

Cable patt
(**Note**: Marker is moved 3 sts on round 18 and returns to original position on round 20).

Round 1 (RS): *C4L, K6, C4R, rep from * to marker.

Round 2: *K4, P6, K4, rep from * to marker.

Round 3: *K1, C4L, K4, C4R, K1, rep from * to marker.

Round 4: *K5, P4, K5, rep from * to marker.

Round 5: *K2, C4L, K2, C4R, K2, rep from * to marker.

Round 6: *K6, P2, K6, rep from * to marker.

Round 7: *K3, C4L, C4R, K3, rep from * to marker.

Round 8: Knit to marker.

Round 9. *K4, wrap next 6 sts (by slipping next 6 sts from left needle onto CN and hold at front of work, take the yarn clockwise around these 6 sts 3 times, then K6 from CN), K4, rep from * to marker.

Round 10: As round 8.

Round 11: *K3, C4R, C4L, K3, rep from * to marker.

Round 12: As round 6.

Round 13: *K2, C4R, K2, C4L, K2, rep from * to marker.

Round 14: As round 4.

Round 15: *K1, C4R, K4, C4L, K1, rep from * to marker.

Round 16: As round 2.

Round 17: *C4R, K6, C4L, rep from * to marker.

Round 18: *K3, P8, K3, rep from * to marker, then K first 3 sts of this round again and re-position marker after last st knitted.

Round 19: *K8, wrap next 6 sts, rep from * to marker.

Round 20: *P8, K6, rep from * to within 14 sts of marker, P8, K3, now slip the next 3 sts from left needle to right needle, remove marker, slip the 3 sts that you have just slipped back from right needle to left needle then reposition marker after last st knitted.

These 20 rounds form patt.
Work in patt for a further 37 rounds, ending after patt round 17.

Next round: *(K2tog) twice, K6, (K2tog) twice, rep from * to marker. 140 sts.

Next round (RS): Purl to marker.

Next round: Knit to marker. Rep last 2 rounds twice more.
BO purlwise.

FINISHING

Block to measurements carefully following instructions on ball band.

17

Oak Leaf Scarf

This uses a variety of tiny to large cables on a reverse stocking stitch background to make the leaves stand proud. Double moss stitch frames the edges.

SIZE
8 in (20 cm) wide and 96½ in (245 cm) long

ABBREVIATIONS
See inside front flap

SPECIAL ABBREVIATION

Cr2B slip next st onto CN and leave at back of work, K1, then K1 from CN

Cr2F slip next st onto CN and leave at front of work, K1, then K1 from CN

Cr3B slip next 2 sts onto CN and leave at back of work, K1, then K2 from CN

Cr3F slip next st onto CN and leave at front of work, K2, then K1 from CN

Cr4B slip next 3 sts onto CN and leave at back of work, K1, then K3 from CN

Cr4F slip next st onto CN and leave at front of work, K3, then K1 from CN

Cr5B slip next 4 sts onto CN and leave at back of work, K1, then K4 from CN

Cr5F slip next st onto CN and leave at front of work, K4, then K1 from CN

MATERIALS NEEDED

DMC Woolly (136 yd/125 m per 50g ball)
8 x Rust (115)
- US 6 (4 mm) needles
- Cable needle

GAUGE (TENSION)

29 sts and 32 rows to 4 in (10 cm) measured patt using US 6 (4 mm) needles.

SCARF

Using US 6 (4 mm) needles CO 56 sts.

Row 1 (RS): K3, P2, *K2, P2, rep from * to last 3 sts, K3.

Row 2: K1, *P2, K2, rep from * to last 3 sts, P2, K1.
Rep the last 2 rows 5 times more, increasing 3 sts evenly across last row and ending with RS facing for next row. 59 sts.
Main patt

Row 1 (RS): K1, (P1, K1) twice, P6, (K1, P4, K9, P4) twice, K1, P6, (K1, P1) twice, K1.

Row 2: P1, (K1, P1) twice, K6, (P1, K4, P9, K4) twice, P1, K6, (P1, K1) twice, P1.

Row 3: P1, (K1, P1) twice, P6, (K1, P5, Cr3B, K1, Cr3F, P5) twice, K1, P6, (K1, P1) twice, P1.

Row 4: K1, (P1, K1) twice, K6, (P1, K6, P5, K6) twice, P1, K6, (K1, P1) twice, K1.

Row 5: K1, (P1, K1) twice, P6, (K1, P6, K5, P6) twice, K1, P6, (K1, P1) twice, K1.

Row 6: P1, (K1, P1) twice, (K1, P11, K1, P5) twice, K1, P11, K1, (P1, K1) twice, P1.

Row 7: P1, (K1, P1) twice, (P1, Cr5B, K1, Cr5F, P1, Cr2B, K1, Cr2F), twice, P1, Cr5B, K1, Cr5F, P1, (P1, K1) twice, P1.

Row 8: K1, (P1, K1) twice, K1, (P11, K3, P1, K3) twice, P11, K1, (K1, P1) twice, K1.

Row 9: K1, (P1, K1) twice, P1, (K11, P3, K1, P3) twice, K11, P1, (K1, P1) twice, K1.

Row 10: P1, (K1, P1) twice, K1, (P11, K3, P1, K3) twice, P11, K1, (P1, K1) twice, P1.

Row 11: P1, (K1, P1) twice, P1, (K11, P3, K1, P3) twice, K11, P1, (P1, K1) twice, P1.

Row 12: K1, (P1, K1) twice, K1, (P11, K3, P1, K3) twice, P11, K1, (K1, P1) twice, K1.

Row 13: K1, (P1, K1) twice, P2, (Cr4B, K1, Cr4F, P4, K1, P4) twice, Cr4B, K1, Cr4F, P2, (K1, P1) twice, K1.

Row 14: P1, (K1, P1) twice, K2, (P9, K4, P1, K4) twice, P9, K2, (P1, K1) twice, P1.

Row 15: P1, (K1, P1) twice, P2, (K9, P4, K1, P4) twice, K9, P2, (P1, K1) twice, P1.

Row 16: K1, (P1, K1) twice, K2, (P9, K4, P1, K4) twice, P9, K2, (K1, P1) twice, K1.

Row 17: K1, (P1, K1) twice, P3, (Cr3B, K1, Cr3F, P5, K1, P5) twice, Cr3B, K1, Cr3F, P3, (K1, P1) twice, K1.

Row 18: P1, (K1, P1) twice, K4, (P5, K6, P1, K6) twice, P5, K4, (P1, K1) twice, P1.

Row 19: P1, (K1, P1) twice, P4, (K5, P6, K1, P6) twice, K5, P4, (P1, K1) twice, P1.

Row 20: K1, (P1, K1) twice, K4, (P5, K1, P11, K1) twice, P5, K4, (K1, P1) twice, K1.

Row 21: K1, (P1, K1) twice, P4, (Cr2B, K1, Cr2F, P1, Cr5B, K1, Cr5F, P1) twice, Cr2B, K1, Cr2F, P4, (K1, P1) twice, K1.

Row 22: P1, (K1, P1) twice, K6, (P1, K3, P11, K3) twice, P1, K6, (P1, K1) twice, P1.

Row 23: P1, (K1, P1) twice, P6, (K1, P3, K11, P3) twice, K1, P6, (P1, K1) twice, P1.

Row 24: K1, (P1, K1) twice, K6, (P1, K3, P11, K3) twice, P1, K6, (K1, P1) twice, K1.

Row 25: K1, (P1, K1) twice, P6, (K1, P3, K11, P3) twice, K1, P6, (K1, P1) twice, K1.

Row 26: P1, (K1, P1) twice, K6, (P1, K3, P11, K3) twice, P1, K6, (P1, K1) twice, P1.

Row 27: P1, (K1, P1) twice, P6, (K1, P4, Cr4B, K1, Cr4F, P4) twice, K1, P6, (P1, K1) twice, P1.

Row 28: K1, (P1, K1) twice, K6, (P1, K4, P9, K4) twice, P1, K6, (K1, P1) twice, K1.

These 28 rows form main patt.
Cont in main patt until scarf meas approx 94½ in (240 cm), ending with RS facing for next row.

Row 1 (RS): K3, P2, *K2, P2, rep from * to last 3 sts, K3.

Row 2: K1, *P2, K2, rep from * to last 3 sts, P2, K1.
Rep the last 2 rows 5 times more, ending with RS facing for next row.
BO in rib.

FINISHING

Block to measurements carefully following instructions on ball band.

18

Summer Feather and Fan Scarf

Delicate and light. This is knitted in cotton for a summer feel. The two color lace stitch is open and has an airy look, created by the wave effect.

SIZE
4 ¾ in (12 cm) wide and 78 ¾ in (200 cm) long

ABBREVIATIONS
See inside front flap

MATERIALS NEEDED

DMC Natura Just Cotton Medium (82 yd/75 m per 50g ball)
2 x Elephant (12) **A**
2 x Blanc (01) **B**
• US 7 (4.5 mm) needles

GAUGE (TENSION)

20 sts and 24 rows to 4 in (10 cm) measured over patt using US 7 (4.5 mm) needles.

SCARF

Using US 7 (4.5 mm) needles and yarn **A** CO 24 sts.
Work in g st for 2 rows, ending with RS facing for next row.
Change to yarn **B**.

Main patt
Row 1 (RS): K1, *(K2tog) twice, yo, (K1, yo) 3 times, (skpo) twice, rep from * to last st, K1.

Row 2: K1, P to last st, K1.

Rows 3 and 4: Knit.
Change to yarn **A**.

Row 5: K1, *(K2tog) twice, yo, (K1, yo) 3 times, (skpo) twice, rep from * to last st, K1.

Row 6: K1, P to last st, K1.

Rows 7 and 8: Knit.

Change to yarn **B**.
These 8 rows form patt.
Cont in main patt until scarf meas approx 78¾ in (200 cm), ending with patt row 4 and RS facing for next row.
Change to yarn **A**.
Work in g st for 3 rows, ending with **WS** facing for next row.
BO knitwise (on **WS**) using yarn **A**.

FINISHING

Block to measurements carefully following instructions on ball band.

19

Diamond Neck Warmer

Large striking cables with twisted cables around the outside and double rib border.

SIZE
6½ in (17 cm) wide and 38 in (96 cm) long

ABBREVIATIONS
See inside front flap

SPECIAL ABBREVIATION
C3B slip next st onto CN and leave at back of work, K2, then K1 from CN
C3F slip next 2 sts onto CN and leave at front of work, K1, then K2 from CN
Cr3R slip next st onto CN and leave at back of work, K2, then P1 from CN
Cr3L slip next 2 sts onto CN and leave at front of work, P1, then K2 from CN
C5B slip next 3 sts onto CN and leave at back of work, K2, then K3 from CN

MATERIALS NEEDED
DMC Woolly (136 yd/125 m per 50g ball) 3 x Cream (03)
US 6 (4 mm) needles
• US 6 (4 mm) circular needle
• Cable needle

GAUGE (TENSION)
23 sts and 29 rows to 4 in (10 cm) measured over st st using US 6 (4 mm) needles.

NECK WARMER

Using US 6 (4 mm) needles CO 15 sts.

Next row (WS): K1, P4, K2, P1, K2, P4, K1.

Shape first end as folls:

Row 1 (RS): K5, P2, M1, K1, M1, P2, K5. 17 sts.

Row 2: K1, P4, K2, P3, K2, P4, K1.

Row 3: K1, C4B, P2, M1, K3, M1, P2, C4F, K1. 19 sts.

Row 4: K1, P4, K2, P5, K2, P4, K1.

Row 5: K5, M1P, P2, C5B, P2, M1P, K5. 21 sts.

Row 6: K1, P4, K3, P5, K3, P4, K1.

Row 7: K1, C4B, M1P, P2, C3B, P1, C3F, P2, M1P, C4F, K1. 23 sts.

Row 8: K1, P4, K3, P3, K1, P3, K3, P4, K1.

Row 9: K5, M1P, P2, C3B, P1, K1, P1, C3F, P2, M1P, K5. 25 sts.

Row 10: K1, P4, K3, P3, K1, P1, K1, P3, K3, P4, K1.

Row 11: K1, C4B, M1P, P2, C3B, (P1, K1) twice, P1, C3F, P2, M1P, C4F, K1. 27 sts.

Row 12: K1, P4, K3, P3, (K1, P1) twice, K1, P3, K3, P4, K1.

Row 13: K5, M1P, P2, C3B, (P1, K1) 3 times, P1, C3F, P2, M1P, K5. 29 sts.

Row 14: K1, P4, K3, P3, (K1, P1) 3 times, K1, P3, K3, P4, K1.

Row 15: K1, C4B, M1P, P2, C3B, (P1, K1) 4 times, P1, C3F, P2,

M1P, C4F, K1. 31 sts.

Row 16: K1, P4, K3, P3, (K1, P1) 4 times, K1, P3, K3, P4, K1.

Row 17: K5, M1P, P2, C3B, (P1, K1) 5 times, P1, C3F, P2, M1P, K5. 33 sts.

Row 18: K1, P4, K3, P3, (K1, P1) 5 times, K1, P3, K3, P4, K1.

Row 19: K1, C4B, M1P, P2, C3B, (P1, K1) 6 times, P1, C3F, P2, M1P, C4F, K1. 35 sts.

Row 20: K1, P4, K3, P3, (K1, P1) 6 times, K1, P3, K3, P4, K1.

Row 21: K5, P2, C3B, (P1, K1) 7 times, P1, C3F, P2, K5.

Row 22: K1, P4, K2, P3, (K1, P1) 7 times, K1, P3, K2, P4, K1.

Row 23: K1, C4B, P2, K2, (P1, K1) 8 times, P1, K2, P2, C4F, K1.

Row 24: K1, P4, K2, P2, (K1, P1) 8 times, K1, P2, K2, P4, K1.

Row 25: K5, P2, Cr3L, (P1, K1) 7 times, P1, Cr3R, P2, K5.

Row 26: K1, P4, K3, P2, (K1, P1) 7 times, K1, P2, K3, P4, K1.

Main patt

Row 1 (RS): K1, C4B, P3, Cr3L, (P1, K1) 6 times, P1, Cr3R, P3, C4F, K1.

Row 2: K1, P4, K4, P2, (K1, P1) 6 times, K1, P2, K4, P4, K1.

Row 3: K5, P4, Cr3L, (P1, K1) 5 times, P1, Cr3R, P4, K5.

Row 4: K1, P4, K5, P2, (K1, P1) 5 times, K1, P2, K5, P4, K1.

Row 5: K1, C4B, P5, Cr3L, (P1, K1) 4 times, P1, Cr3R, P5, C4F, K1.

Row 6: K1, P4, K6, P2, (K1, P1) 4 times, K1, P2, K6, P4, K1.

Row 7: K5, P6, Cr3L, (P1, K1) 3 times, P1, Cr3R, P6, K5.

Row 8: K1, P4, K7, P2, (K1, P1) 3 times, K1, P2, K7, P4, K1.

Row 9: K1, C4B, P7, Cr3L, (P1, K1) twice, P1, Cr3R, P7, C4F, K1.

Row 10: K1, P4, K8, P2, (K1, P1) twice, K1, P2, K8, P4, K1.

Row 11: K5, P8, Cr3L, P1, K1, P1, Cr3R, P8, K5.

Row 12: K1, P4, K9, P2, K1, P1, K1, P2, K9, P4, K1.

Row 13: K1, C4B, P9, Cr3L, P1, Cr3R, P9, C4F, K1.

Row 14: K1, P4, K10, P2, K1, P2, K10, P4, K1.

Row 15: K5, P10, C5B, P10, K5.

Row 16: K1, P4, K10, P5, K10, P4, K1.

Row 17: K1, C4B, P9, C3B, P1, C3F, P9, C4F, K1.

Row 18: K1, P4, K9, P3, K1, P3, K9, P4, K1.

Row 19: K5, P8, C3B, P1, K1, P1, C3F, P8, K5.

Row 20: K1, P4, K8, P3, K1, P1, K1, P3, K8, P4, K1.

Row 21: K1, C4B, P7, C3B, (P1, K1) twice, P1, C3F, P7, C4F, K1.

Row 22: K1, P4, K7, P3, (K1, P1) twice, K1, P3, K7, P4, K1.

Row 23: K5, P6, C3B, (P1, K1) 3 times, P1, C3F, P6, K5.

Row 24: K1, P4, K6, P3, (K1, P1) 3 times, K1, P3, K6, P4, K1.

Row 25: K1, C4B, P5, C3B, (P1, K1) 4 times, P1, C3F, P5, C4F, K1.

Row 26: K1, P4, K5, P3, (K1, P1) 4 times, K1, P3, K5, P4, K1.

Row 27: K5, P4, C3B, (P1, K1) 5 times, P1, C3F, P4, K5.

Row 28: K1, P4, K4, P3, (K1, P1) 5 times, K1, P3, K4, P4, K1.

Row 29: K1, C4B, P3, C3B, (P1, K1) 6 times, P1, C3F, P3, C4F, K1.

Row 30: K1, P4, K3, P3, (K1, P1) 6 times, K1, P3, K3, P4, K1.

Row 31: K5, P2, C3B, (P1, K1) 7 times, P1, C3F, P2, K5.

Row 32: K1, P4, K2, P3, (K1, P1) 7 times, K1, P3, K2, P4, K1.

Row 33: K1, C4B, P2, K2, (P1, K1) 8 times, P1, K2, P2, C4F, K1.

Row 34: K1, P4, K2, P2, (K1, P1) 8 times, K1, P2, K2, P4, K1.

Row 35: K5, P2, Cr3L, (P1, K1) 7 times, P1, Cr3R, P2, K5.

Row 36: K1, P4, K3, P2, (K1, P1) 7 times, K1, P2, K3, P4, K1.
These 36 rows form patt.
Rep these 36 patt rows 5 times more, ending with RS facing for next row.

Shape second end as folls:

Row 1 (RS): K1, C4B, P2tog, P1, Cr3L, (P1, K1) 6 times, P1, Cr3R, P1, P2tog tbl, C4F, K1. 33 sts.

Row 2: K1, P4, K3, P2, (K1, P1) 6 times, K1, P2, K3, P4, K1.

Row 3: K5, P2tog, P1, Cr3L, (P1, K1) 5 times, P1, Cr3R, P1, P2tog tbl, K5. 31 sts.

Row 4: K1, P4, K3, P2, (K1, P1) 5 times, K1, P2, K3, P4, K1.

Row 5: K1, C4B, P2tog, P1, Cr3L, (P1, K1) 4 times, P1, Cr3R, P1, P2tog tbl, C4F, K1. 29 sts.

Row 6: K1, P4, K3, P2, (K1, P1) 4 times, K1, P2, K3, P4, K1.

Row 7: K5, P2tog, P1, Cr3L, (P1, K1) 3 times, P1, Cr3R, P1, P2tog tbl, K5. 27 sts.

Row 8: K1, P4, K3, P2, (K1, P1) 3 times, K1, P2, K3, P4, K1.

Row 9: K1, C4B, P2tog, P1, Cr3L, (P1, K1) twice, P1, Cr3R, P1, P2tog tbl, C4F, K1. 25 sts.

Row 10: K1, P4, K3, P2, (K1, P1) twice K1, P2, K3, P4, K1.

Row 11: K5, P2tog, P1, Cr3L, P1, K1, P1, Cr3R, P1, P2tog tbl, K5. 23 sts.

Row 12: K1, P4, K3, P2, K1, P1, K1, P2, K3, P4, K1.

Row 13: K1, C4B, P2tog, P1, Cr3L, P1, Cr3R, P1, P2tog tbl, C4F, K1. 21 sts.

Row 14: K1, P4, K3, P2, K1, P2, K3, P4, K1.

Row 15: K5, P2tog, P1, C5B, P1, P2tog tbl, K5. 19 sts.

Row 16: K1, P4, K2, P5, K2, P4, K1.

Row 17: K1, C4B, P2, K2tog, skpo, K1, P2, C4F, K1. 17 sts.

Row 18: K1, P4, K2, P3, K2, P4, K1.

Row 19: K5, P2, sl 2 as if to K2tog, K1, p2sso, P2, K5. 15 sts. BO in patt (on **WS**).

BORDER

Fold neck warmer in half so that CO and BO edges are together and place a marker at centre of the straight edge. This marker will be centre back neck edge.

Using US 6 (4 mm) circular needle pick up and knit 72 sts evenly from marker to start of curve, 42 sts around curve, 144 sts along straight edge to start of curve, 42 sts around curve then 72 sts to marker. 372 sts.
Place marker and join for working in the round, taking care not to twist the knitting.

Rounds 1 to 3: *K2, P1, rep from * to end.

Round 4: *K2, Pfb, rep from * to end. 496 sts.

Rounds 5 to 9: *K2, P2, rep from * to end.

Round 10: *K2, P1, Pfb, rep from * to end. 620 sts. BO in patt.

FINISHING

Soak neck warmer in warm water and then remove excess water by pressing in a towel and leave to dry flat. Tie neck warmer to fasten as shown in photograph.

20

Fisherman's Rib and Garter Stitch Scarf

A close knit woven effect, made up of horizontal garter stitch blocks and vertical blocks of Fisherman's rib, creating a great scarf for a man.

SIZE
8 in (20 cm) wide and 62 in (160 cm) long

ABBREVIATIONS
See inside front flap

MATERIALS NEEDED
DMC Woolly (136 yd/125 m per 50g ball)
6 x Charcoal (123)
• US 6 (4 mm) needles

GAUGE (TENSION)
23 sts and 30 rows to 4 in (10 cm) measured over patt using US 6 (4 mm) needles.

SCARF
Using US 6 (4 mm) needles CO 47 sts.

Row 1 (RS): Knit.

Row 2: (K1, P1 below) 5 times, *K9, (P1 below, K1) 4 times, P1 below, rep from * once more, K1.

Rows 3 to 16: As rows 1 and 2, 7 times.

Row 17: Knit.

Row 18: K10, *P1 below, (K1, P1 below) 4 times, K9, rep from * once more, K1.

Rows 19 to 32: As rows 17 and 18, 7 times.
These 32 rows form patt.
Continue in patt until scarf meas approx 62 in (160 cm), ending with patt row 16 and RS facing for next row.
BO knitwise.

FINISHING
Block to measurements carefully following instructions on ball band.

21

Pompom Shawl

Knitted entirely in garter stitch this shawl starts at one end and gently increases to give a broad shape around the shoulders. The bright color of the pompoms keep the shawl in place while adding a pop of color.

SIZE
22 ¾ in (58 cm) at widest part and 67 in (170 cm) long

ABBREVIATIONS
See inside front flap

MATERIALS NEEDED
DMC Woolly (136 yd/125 m per 50g ball)
5 x Cream (03) **A**
1 x Lipstick (055) **B**
• US 5 (3.75 mm) needles

GAUGE (TENSION)
25 sts and 48 rows to 4 in (10 cm) measured over g st using US 5 (3.75 mm) needles.

SHAWL
Using US 5 (3.75 mm) needles and yarn **A** CO 4 sts.
Work in g st for 84 rows, ending with RS facing for next row.

Next row (RS): K to last 2 sts, M1, K2.

Next row: Knit.
Rep the last 2 rows until there are 134 sts and ending with RS facing for next row.
Work in g st for 2 rows.

Next row (RS): K to last 4 sts, K2tog, K2.

Next row: Knit.
Rep the last 2 rows until 4 sts rem, ending with **WS** facing for next row.
Work in g st for 85 rows, ending with RS facing for next row.
BO.

FINISHING

Block to measurements carefully following instructions on ball band. Using yarn **B** make two 4 in (10 cm) pompoms. Using photograph as a guide attach a pompom to each end of CO and BO edge as shown.

22

Double Seed and Garter Stitch Scarf

Long bands of rib and garter stitch are interspaced with double seed stitch which combine to give long clean lines.

SIZE

8½ in (22 cm) wide and 74¾ in (190 cm) long

ABBREVIATIONS

See inside front flap

MATERIALS NEEDED

DMC Woolly (136 yd/125 m per 50g ball)
5 x Brown (113)
• US 6 (4 mm) needles

GAUGE (TENSION)

25 sts and 34 rows to 4 in (10 cm) measured over patt using US 6 (4 mm) needles.

SCARF

Using US 6 (4 mm) needles CO 55 sts.

Row 1 (RS): K5, *P1, (K1, P1) twice, K5, rep from * to end.

Row 2: *P1, K3, (P1, K1) 3 times, rep from * to last 5 sts, P1, K3, P1.

Row 3: K5, *(K1, P1) twice, K6, rep from * to end.

Row 4: P1, K3, P1, *(P1, K1) twice, P2, K3, P1, rep from * to end.

These 4 rows form patt.
Cont in patt until scarf meas 74¾ in (190 cm), ending with RS facing for next row.
BO in patt.

FINISHING

Block to measurements carefully following instructions on ball band.

23

Braided Scarf

An intricate pattern which combines a variety of cable stitches to form a dense braided pattern. Plaits and twists are interwoven to create a stunning cable design.

SIZE
6 ¼ in (16 cm) wide and 78 ¾ in (200 cm) long

ABBREVIATIONS
See inside front flap

SPECIAL ABBREVIATIONS
Cr4R slip next st onto CN and leave at back of work, K3, then P1 from CN
Cr4L slip next 3 sts onto CN and leave at front of work, P1, then K3 from CN
C6B slip next 3 sts onto CN and leave at back of work, K3, then K3 from CN
C6F slip next 3 sts onto CN and leave at front of work, K3, then K3 from CN
Cr6R slip next 3 sts onto CN and leave at back of work, K3, then P3 from CN
Cr6L slip next 3 sts onto CN and leave at front of work, P3, then K3 from CN

MATERIALS NEEDED
DMC Woolly (136 yd/125 m per 50g ball)
6 x Fuchsia (054)
- US 6 (4 mm) needles
- Cable needle

GAUGE (TENSION)
32 sts and 34 rows to 4 in (10 cm) measured patt using US 6 (4 mm) needles.

SCARF

Using US 6 (4 mm) needles CO 46 sts.

Next row (WS): (Pfb) 3 times, P3, K5, (Pfb) 3 times, P3, K3, (Pfb) 6 times, K3, P3, (Pfb) 3 times, K5, P3, (Pfb) 3 times. 64 sts.

Row 1 (RS): C6F, K3, P5, C6B, K3, P3, (C6F) twice, P3, K3, C6F, P5, K3, C6B.

Row 2: P9, K5, P9, K3, P12, K3, P9, K5, P9.

Row 3: K9, P4, Cr4R, C6F, Cr6R, K6, Cr6L, C6B, Cr4L, P4, K9.

Row 4: P9, K4, P3, K1, P9, K3, P6, K3, P9, K1, P3, K4, P9.

Row 5: K3, C6B, P3, Cr4R, P1, K3, C6B, P3, C6B, P3, C6F, K3, P1, Cr4L, P3, C6F, K3.

Row 6: P9, K3, P3, K2, P9, K3, P6, K3, P9, K2, P3, K3, P9.

Row 7: K9, P2, Cr4R, P2, C6F, K3, P3, K6, P3, K3, C6B, P2, Cr4L, P2, K9.

Row 8: P9, K2, P3, K3, P9, K3, P6, K3, P9, K3, P3, K2, P9.

Row 9: C6F, K3, P2, K3, P3, K3, C6B, P3, C6B, P3, C6F, K3, P3, K3, P2, K3, C6B.

Row 10: As row 8.

Row 11: K9, P2, Cr4L, P2, C6F, K3, P3, K6, P3, K3, C6B, P2, Cr4R, P2, K9.

Row 12: As row 6.

Row 13: K3, C6B, P3, Cr4L, P1, K3, (C6B, P3) twice, C6F, K3, P1, Cr4R, P3, C6F, K3.

Row 14: As row 4.

Row 15: K9, P4, Cr4L, C6F, Cr6L, K6, Cr6R, C6B, Cr4R, P4, K9.

Row 16: As row 2.
These 16 rows form patt.

Cont in patt until work meas approx 78¾ in (200 cm), ending with patt row 1 and **WS** facing for next row.

Next row (WS): (P2tog) 3 times, P3, K5, (P2tog) 3 times, P3, K3, (P2tog) 6 times, K3, P3, (P2tog) 3 times, K5, P3, (P2tog) 3 times. 46 sts.
BO in patt.

FINISHING

Block to measurements carefully following instructions on ball band.

24

Ruffle Edged Shawl

A garter stitch triangle is bordered by a simple but elegant neat ruffle by alternating stocking stitch with reversing stocking stitch and the use of simple short-row shaping.

SIZE

12 ½ in (32 cm) at widest part and 59 ¼ in (150 cm) long

ABBREVIATIONS

See inside front flap

MATERIALS NEEDED

DMC Woolly (136 yd/125 m per 50g ball)
4 x Purple (065)
• US 5 (3.75 mm) needles

GAUGE (TENSION)

25 sts and 48 rows to 4 in (10 cm) measured over g st using US 5 (3.75 mm) needles.

SHAWL

Using US 5 (3.75 mm) needles CO 9 sts, place a marker, then CO a further 2 sts. 11 sts.

Row 1 (RS): K to marker, slip marker, K9.

Row 2: P9, turn. K9, turn.

Row 3: P9, slip marker, K to end.

Row 4: K to marker, M1, slip marker, P9.

Row 5: K9, turn. P9, turn.

Row 6: K9, slip marker, K to end.
These 6 rows form patt.
Cont as set until there are 68 sts in g st on the right side of marker, ending on row 6 of patt and with RS facing for next row.

Row 1 (RS): K to marker, slip marker, K9.

Row 2: P9, turn. K9, turn.

Row 3: P9, slip marker, K to end.

Row 4: K to 2 sts before marker, K2tog, slip marker, P9.

Row 5: K9, turn. P9, turn.

Row 6: K9, slip marker, K to end.

These 6 rows form patt.
Cont as set until there are 2 sts in g st on the left side of marker, ending on row 6 of patt and with RS facing for next row. BO.

FINISHING

Block to measurements carefully following instructions on ball band.

25

Pompom Scarf

Large bands of garter stitch and moss stitch form this scarf which is embellished with large brightly colored pompoms on the moss stitch sections.

SIZE
8¼ in (21 cm) wide and 78¾ in (200 cm) long

ABBREVIATIONS
See inside front flap

MATERIALS NEEDED
DMC Natura Just Cotton XL (82 yd/75 m per 50g ball)
5 x Ecru (03) **A**

- **DMC Woolly** (136 yd/125 m per 50g ball)
  1 x Cream (03) **B**
  1 x Fondant (043) **C**
  1 x Red (052) **D**
  1 x Mauve (063) **E**
  1 x Turquoise (074) **F**
  1 x Royal (075) **G**
  1 x Avocado (081) **H**
  1 x Yellow (093) **I**
  1 x Orange (102) **J**

- US 10 (6 mm) needles

GAUGE (TENSION)
12 sts and 24 rows to 4 in (10 cm) measured over patt using US 10 (6 mm) needles.

SCARF
Using US 10 (6 mm) needles and yarn **A** CO 25 sts.
Work in g st until scarf meas 15¾ in (40 cm), ending with RS facing for next row.

Next row (RS): K1, *P1, K1, rep from * to end.
Last row forms patt.
Cont in patt until scarf meas 63 in (160 cm), from CO edge, ending with RS facing for next row.
Work in g st until scarf meas 78¾ in (200 cm), from CO edge, ending with **WS** facing for next row.
BO knitwise (on **WS**).

FINISHING
Sew in all loose ends.
Cover with a damp cloth and leave to dry naturally.
Make random colored and sized pompoms using yarns **C**, **D**, **E**, **F**, **G**, **H**, **I** and **J** tie the centre of each pompom using yarn **B** leaving a 6 in (15 cm) yarn tail, use photo as a guide, attach the pompoms using the end as shown.

26

Simple Buttoned Cowl

Knitted in sections for a modern look, this seed stitch cowl is fastened at the side with decorative buttons.

SIZE

7½ in (19 cm) wide and 25½ in (65 cm) long

ABBREVIATIONS

See inside front flap

MATERIALS NEEDED

DMC Natura Just Cotton Medium (82 yd/75 m per 50 g ball)
3 x Tagliatelle (31)
- US 6 (4 mm) needles
- 3 buttons

GAUGE (TENSION)

17 sts and 32 rows to 4 in (10 cm) measured over seed (moss) stitch using US 6 (4 mm) needles.

COWL

FIRST FLAP

****Using US 6 (4 mm) needles CO 10 sts.
Work in g st for 2 rows, ending with RS facing for next row.

Next row (RS): K3, K2tog, (yo) twice, skpo, K3.

Next row: Knit, working (K1, K1 tbl) into double yo on previous row.
Work in g st for 2 rows, inc 1 st at centre on last row and ending with RS facing for next row. 11 sts. ****

Next row (RS): K1, *P1, K1, rep from * to end.
Last row forms patt.
Work a further 17 rows in patt, ending with RS facing for next row.
Cut off yarn and leave these 11 sts on a holder.

SECOND FLAP

Work as given for first flap from ** to ** then work as folls:

Row 1 (RS): P1, *K1, P1, rep from * to end.
Last row forms patt.
Work a further 7 rows in patt, ending with RS facing for next row.
Cut off yarn and leave these 11 sts on a holder.

THIRD FLAP

Work as given for first flap from ** to ** then work as folls:

Next row (RS): K1, *P1, K1, rep from * to end.
Last row forms patt.
Work a further 7 rows in patt, ending with RS facing for next row.
Do not cut yarn.

FIRST JOINING SECTION

Note: you will only be joining third and second flap together.

Next row (RS): With RS facing work across third flap as folls: K1, (P1, K1) 5 times, then with RS facing work across second flap as folls: P1, (K1, P1) 5 times. 22 sts.

Next row (WS): *P1, K1, rep from * to end.

Next row: *K1, P1, rep from * to end.
Last 2 rows form patt.
Cont in patt for a further 7 rows, ending with RS facing for next row.

SECOND JOINING SECTION

Note: you will now be joining all three flaps together.

Next row (RS): (K1, P1) 11 times, then with RS facing work across first flap as folls: K1, (P1, K1) 5 times. 33 sts.

Next row (WS): K1, *P1, K1, rep from * to end.
Last row forms patt.
Cont in patt until work meas 25½ in (65 cm) from CO edge, ending with RS facing for next row.

Next row (RS): Knit, dec 3 sts evenly. 30 sts.
Work in g st for 4 rows, ending with **WS** facing for next row.
BO knitwise (on **WS**).

FINISHING

Block to measurements carefully following instructions on ball band. Sew on buttons to correspond with buttonholes.

27
Lace and Cable Edged Shawl

An elongated triangular shaped design in garter stitch, bordered with an elegant twisted cable and pointed zig-zagged lace.

SIZE
13¾ in (35 cm) at widest point and 78¾ in (200 cm) long

ABBREVIATIONS
See inside front flap

SPECIAL ABBREVIATIONS

C4B slip next 2 sts onto CN and hold at back of work, K2, then K2 from CN

sm slip marker

MATERIALS NEEDED

DMC Woolly (136 yd/125 m per 50g ball)
6 x Turquoise (074)
- US 5 (3.75 mm) needles
- Cable needle

GAUGE (TENSION)

25 sts and 48 rows to 4 in (10 cm) measured over g st using US 5 (3.75 mm) needles.

SHAWL

Using US 5 (3.75 mm) needles CO 2 sts, place a marker, then CO a further 10 sts. 12 sts.

Row 1 (RS): K1, yo, K2tog, yo, K7, sm, K to end.

Row 2 and every foll alt row: K to marker, sm, P4, K to end.

Row 3: K1, (yo, K2tog) twice, yo, K2, C4B, sm, M1, K to end.

Row 5: K1, (yo, K2tog) twice, yo, K7, sm, K to end.

Row 7: K1, (yo, K2tog) 3 times, yo, K2, C4B, sm, K to end.

Row 9: K1, (yo, K2tog) 3 times, yo, K7, sm, M1, K to end.

Row 11: BO 6 sts knitwise (1 st on right needle), yo, K2tog, yo, K2, C4B, sm, K to end.

Row 12: K to marker, sm, P4, K to end.
These 12 rows form patt.
Cont as set until there are 68 sts in g st on the left side of marker, ending on row 12 of patt and with RS facing for next row.

Row 1 (RS): K1, yo, K2tog, yo, K7, sm, K to end.

Row 2 and every foll alt row: K to marker, sm, P4, K to end.

Row 3: K1, (yo, K2tog) twice, yo, K2, C4B, sm, K2tog tbl, K to end.

Row 5: K1, (yo, K2tog) twice, yo, K7, sm, K to end.

Row 7: K1, (yo, K2tog) 3 times, yo, K2, C4B, sm, K to end.

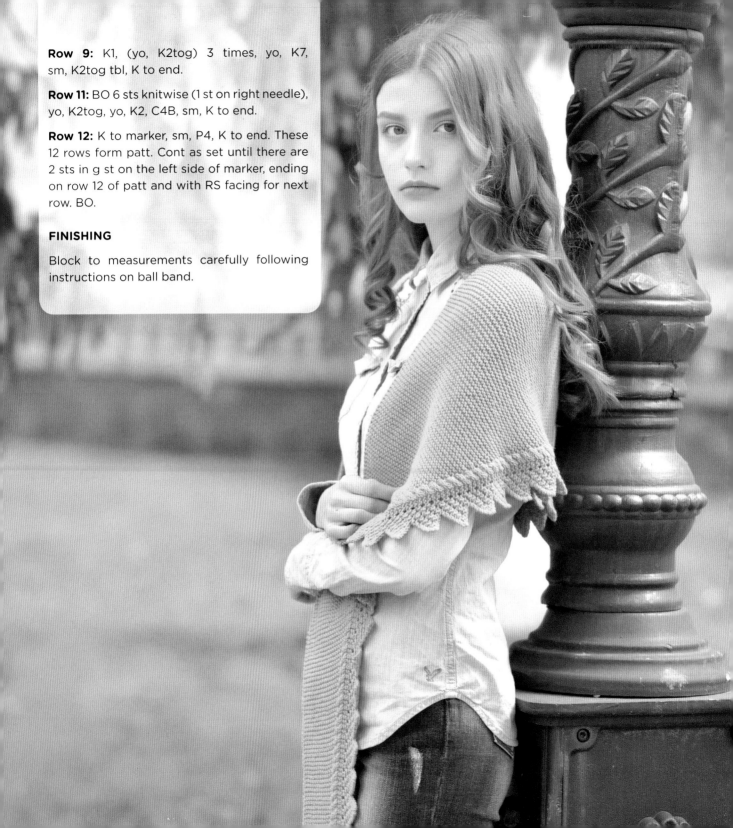

Row 9: K1, (yo, K2tog) 3 times, yo, K7, sm, K2tog tbl, K to end.

Row 11: BO 6 sts knitwise (1 st on right needle), yo, K2tog, yo, K2, C4B, sm, K to end.

Row 12: K to marker, sm, P4, K to end. These 12 rows form patt. Cont as set until there are 2 sts in g st on the left side of marker, ending on row 12 of patt and with RS facing for next row. BO.

FINISHING

Block to measurements carefully following instructions on ball band.

28

Cabled Scarf

Knitting in chunky cotton this scarf has a tight woven cable edged with tassels. Alternating forward and backward cables create this simple but effective design.

SIZE
8¼ in (21 cm) wide and 86½ in (220 cm) long

ABBREVIATIONS
See inside front flap

SPECIAL ABBREVIATIONS

C8B slip next 4 sts onto CN and leave at back of work, K4, then K4 from CN

C8F slip next 4 sts onto CN and leave at front of work, K4, then K4 from CN

MATERIALS NEEDED

DMC Natura Just Cotton XL (82 yd/75 m per 100g ball) 8 x Grey (12)
- US 11 (8 mm) needles
- Cable needle

GAUGE (TENSION)

19 sts and 24 rows to 4 in (10 cm) measured over patt using US 11 (8 mm) needles.

SCARF

Using US 11 (8 mm) needles CO 28 sts.

Next row (WS): K2, *P1, (Pfb) 3 times, P1, rep from * to last 6 sts, P4, K2. 40 sts.

Row 1: Knit.

Row 2: K2, P36, K2.

Row 3: K6, (C8F) 4 times, K2.

Row 4: As row 2.

Rows 5 to 8: As rows 1 and 2 twice.

Row 9: K2, (C8B) 4 times, K6.

Row 10: As row 2.

Rows 11 to 12: As row 1 and 2. These 12 rows form patt. Cont in patt until scarf meas approx 86½ in (220 cm), ending with patt row 5 and **WS** facing for next row.

Next row (WS): K2, *P1, (P2tog) 3 times, P1, rep from * to last 6 sts, P4, K2. 28 sts. BO.

FINISHING

Cover with a damp cloth and leave to dry naturally. Cut several 8 in (20 cm) lengths of yarn. Take 30 lengths of yarn for each tassel and fold in half then using photograph as a guide wrap another length tightly around the fold of the tassel as shown. Attach 5 tassels to each end of scarf.

29

Diamond Cable Scarf

Large diamond cables stand out on a background of garter stitch giving a three dimensional effect. Twisted cables border the design on each side.

SIZE

8 in (20 cm) wide and 67 in (170 cm) long

ABBREVIATIONS

See inside front flap

SPECIAL ABBREVIATIONS

Cr5R slip next 2 sts onto CN and leave at back of work, K3, then P2 from CN.

Cr5L slip next 3 sts onto CN and leave at front of work, P2, then K3 from CN.

C6B slip next 3 sts onto CN and leave at back of work, K3, then K3 from CN.

C6F slip next 3 sts onto CN and leave at front of work, K3, then K3 from CN.

MATERIALS NEEDED

DMC Natura Just Cotton Medium (82 yd/75 m per 50g ball)

7 x Vanille (03)

- US 8 (5 mm) needles
- Cable needle

GAUGE (TENSION)

23 sts and 44 rows to 4 in (10 cm) measured over g st using US 8 (5 mm) needles.

SCARF

Using US 8 (5 mm) needles CO 37 sts.

Next row (WS): K6, (Pfb) 3 times, P8, (Pfb) 3 times, P8, (Pfb) 3 times, K6. 46 sts.

Row 1 (RS): K6, C6B, (P8, C6F) twice, K6.

Row 2 and every foll alt row: K6, P34, K6.

Row 3: K12, P8, K6, P8, K12.

Row 5: As row 1.

Row 7: K12, P6, Cr5R, Cr5L, P6, K12.

Row 9: K6, C6B, P4, Cr5R, P4, Cr5L, P4, C6F, K6.

Row 11: K12, P2, Cr5R, P8, Cr5L, P2, K12.

Row 13: K6, C6B, Cr5R, P12, Cr5L, C6F, K6.

Row 15: K9, C6F, P16, C6B, K9.

Row 17: K6, C6B, Cr5L, P12, Cr5R, C6F, K6.

Row 19: K12, P2, Cr5L, P8, Cr5R, P2, K12.

Row 21: K6, C6B, P4, Cr5L, P4, Cr5R, P4, C6F, K6.

Row 23: K12, P6, Cr5L, Cr5R, P6, K12.

Row 24: As row 2. These 24 rows form patt. Cont in patt until scarf meas approx 67 in (170 cm), ending with row 5 of patt and **WS** facing for next row.

Next row (WS): K6, (P2tog) 3 times, P8, (P2tog) 3 times, P8, (P2tog) 3 times, K6. 37 sts. BO.

FINISHING

Block to measurements carefully following instructions on ball band.

30

Easy Drop Stitch Scarf

A quick to knit scarf using an effective drop stitch technique. Rows of garter stitch separate the dropped loops giving an open and light feel to the scarf.

SIZE

8 in (20 cm) wide and 78¾ in (200 cm) long

ABBREVIATIONS

See inside front flap

MATERIALS NEEDED

DMC Woolly (136 yd/125 m per 50g ball)
8 x Orange (103)
• US 8 (5 mm) needles

GAUGE (TENSION)

18 sts and 22 rows to 4 in (10 cm) measured over patt using US 8 (5 mm) needles and **2 strands** of yarn held together.

SCARF

Using US 8 (5 mm) needles and **2 strands** of yarn held together CO 36 sts.

Rows 1 to 4: Knit.

Row 5 (RS): *K1 wrapping yarn twice round needle, rep from * to end.

Row 6: Knit, dropping extra loops.
Last 6 rows form patt.
Cont in patt until scarf meas approx 78¾ in (200 cm), ending with patt row 3 and **WS** facing for next row.
BO knitwise (on **WS**).

FINISHING

Block to measurements carefully following instructions on ball band.

ABBREVIATIONS

K	knit
P	purl
CO	cast on
BO	bind (cast) off
st(s)	stitch(es)
inc	increas(e)(ing)
dec	decreas(e)(ing)
Pfb	purl into front then back of next stitch
Kfb	knit into front then back of next stitch
st st	stockinette (stocking) stitch (1 row K, 1 row P)
g st	garter stitch (K every row)
Beg	begin(ning)
foll	following
folls	follows
rem	remain(ing)
rep	repeat
alt	alternate
cont	continue
patt	pattern
tog	together
mm	millimeters
cm	centimeter(s)
in	inch(es)
m	meter(s)
yd	yard(s)
g	gram(s)
oz	ounce(s)
RS	right side
WS	wrong side
sl 1	slip one stitch
sl2	slip two stitches
psso	pass slipped stitch over
p2sso	pass 2 slipped stitches over
skpo	slip 1, K1, pass slipped stitch over
P2tog	purl 2 together
K2tog	knit 2 together
tbl	through back loop(s)
yo	yarn over
cn	cable needle
meas	measures
O	no stitches, times or rows
-	no stitches, times or rows for that size
M1	make one stitch by picking up horizontal loop before next stitch and knitting into back of it
M1P	make one stitch by picking up horizontal loop before next stitch and purling into back of it

About the Author

Jody Long was born in Portsmouth, in the United Kingdom. He grew up in Waterlooville, Hampshire, and moved to Málaga, Spain, in 2014. For over twelve years, he designed for all the major U.K. and U.S. knitting magazines, then moved on to design for knitting mills around the globe and writing knitting books. Jody has also designed for celebrity clients.

Jody has a website which is www.jodylongknits.com